WHAT
THE FUSILIERS DID.

AN ACCOUNT

OF THE PART TAKEN BY

THE

1st BATTALION,

5th NORTHUMBERLAND FUSILIERS,

IN THE

AFGHAN CAMPAIGNS

OF

1878-79 and 1879-80.

BY

PRIVATE H. COOPER,
Of the above Regiment.

Lahore:

1880.

DEAR COMRADES,

When I wrote the following pages, I wrote them for the information of a few friends at home and had no idea of getting them printed ; and it was only at the request of many men of the regiment that I consented to send them to the Press. I have written them as plain and straightforward as I possibly could, and have endeavoured to give a true and complete account of what we have gone through from the time of leaving Chakrata in 1878 till our arrival in Lawrencepore in 1880.

Hoping that what I have written may be appreciated,

I remain,

Your affectionate comrade,

H. C.

WHAT THE FUSILIERS DID.

PRELUDE.

Come Britons all and list to me, while I relate to you
  Of daring deeds most nobly done, by a regiment staunch and true,
This regiment is the gallant Fifth Northumberland Fusiliers,
  Who for Old England well have fought for o'er 200 years.

In many climes, both hot and cold, have they their duty done,
  And 'gainst Old England's enemies great victories have won.
In every fight that they've fought they always stood their ground ;
  Their equals on the battle field they never yet have found.

They never from their foemen ran, though they be thousands strong,
  And I am very proud to say that to them I belong.
Our motto, *Quo Fata Vocant*, means "ready when required" ;
  And oft' before our battle cry have enemies retired.

Our Colors, noble emblem of victories, long since gone by,
  For every honor woven there, brave men did nobly die ;
There's Orthes, Toulouse, and Nivelle, and Wilhelmstahl as well,
  Busaco and Corunna, where Sir John Moore nobly fell.

Cuidad Rodrigo, Roleia, and the hard fought Badajorz,
  And Salamanca fatal field, great was the Frenchman's loss ;
We also have Peninsula, where many were laid low,
  Vittoria and Vimiera too, also the famed Lucknow ;
But, its not of these my story is, for they are deeds of old,
  The way in which those days were won has long ago been told.

'Tis of another honor, which on our Colors soon will be :
  Afghanistan that honor is—'twas earned most gallantly ;
To gain it we all fought like men, and many comrades died,
  And when our Colors it adorns, we'll gaze on it with pride.

Then gather round me, one and all, bold Britons near and far,
  Whilst I relate the part we played during the Afghan war ;
A part I hope which will be praised, hundreds of years hence,
  So if you'll now attention give, my story I'll commence.

PART THE FIRST.

For nigh twelve years on India's plains had we our country served,
  Though oft' attacked by foul disease from duty never swerved.
Tho' far away from friends so dear, Old England, home, and beauty;
  Though longing to get back again, we cheerfully did our duty.

Thro' living 'neath a scorching sun our features were tanned brown,
  From long years' of exposure too, our health was breaking down;
When to the hills we all were sent, where we arrived at length,
  The object of our mission was to recruit our health and strength.

Our station was an healthy one, Chackrata it is named,
  Seven thousand feet above the sea, in the Himalayas so famed.
The air was pure, the view was grand, around all was serene.
  The snow clad hills, and lovely vales, formed quite a pleasant scene.

While we were there we had good times, which I think well-earned,
  Before we had been there six months our health again returned.
'Twas well for us that this was so, that sickly men were few,
  For very soon we were to have some hard stern work to do.

For war had once more broken out, which filled our foes with fear,
  Between the Indian Government and the Afghanistan Ameer.
The cause was this, the Ameer had our Government deceived,
  Without our Viceroy's sanction he the Muscovite received.

He welcom'd the Russian Mission, and our Envoy much abused,
  When asked our Mission to receive, he scornfully refused.
He said we could do as we liked, for us he nothing cared,
  So just to bring his senses back, war was at once declared.

Our regiment being in numbers strong, and in good health also,
  On this account we thought that we to the coming war would go.
Nor were we disappointed, for we soon received an order,
  Which said we would shortly march towards the Afghan border.

'Twas on the eighth day of October, eighteen seventy-eight,
  A telegram from Simla came, in which it there did state:
" Warn Fusiliers for service, particulars by post."
  We knew by this we were destined to meet the Afghan host.

This telegram was very short, but satisfaction gave,
  It raised the martial spirit of the Fusiliers so brave.
When it was read, we gave three cheers, and hurrah'd every one,
  For visions came before our eyes of honors to be won.
For were we not to have a chance our country for to serve,
  And, if needs be, to bravely die our Empire to preserve.

Next day when on parade, we were medically inspected,
  When all the boys and sickly men were fell out and rejected.
These men would, had they been allowed, most willingly have gone,
  And with their comrades, as of old, their duty gaily done.
Although they had to stay behind, they did not courage lack,
  They had the will but not the strength : sickness kept them back.

For several days our time we spent, preparing for the fray,
  By getting into fighting trim, and packing things away.
Our surplus kits being in the stores, and all ready as we thought,
  Alas we could not get away, for carriage it was short.

And being anxious for to march, we grumbled at our fate,
  But transport, it was soon procured, we had not long to wait.
And every thing being in its place, all ready for to go,
  The order was we'd march next morn to meet our Afghan foe.

Next morning came, a glorious day, the sun down on us smiled,
  The sky above was azure blue, the atmosphere was mild.
It was the eighteenth of the month, October seventy-eight,
  At six o'clock we all fell in, and not a man was late.

And as we stood there on parade, seven hundred and fifty strong,
  In tunics red and trousers white, we formed a gallant throng.
It was remarked by all our friends, we looked, as we stood there,
  With hair cut short, and whiskers clipped, the warriors we were.

Each man was thoroughly equipped, with bayonet and with rifle,
  Water bottle, and haversack, also another trifle.
This trifle, 'twas seventy rounds of ball ammunition,
  And to his back was neatly strapped his great coat in addition.
The weight of these was very great, three stone I do declare ;
  But as we were the old and bold, of course we didn't care.

The Band, they played Auld Lang Syne (song of the land of Scott),
  Which never fails to bring to mind mem'ries long since forgot.
The married men then bid farewell to wives and children dear,
  And many there were not afraid to shed a manly tear.
For well they knew their absence would these loved ones cause pain,
  And it was possible that they might never meet again.

And now, all leave-takings being o'er, in the ranks stood every man,
  As the Band struck up a lively tune, our journey we began.
And as the station we did leave, we gave three hearty cheers,
  And many a voice was heard to say, God speed the Fusiliers.

For several hours we marched along, with bold and rapid stride,
    Along a dusty, mountain road, and down the steep hill side.
And when we'd gone near fifteen miles, our men began to tire,
    Our Colonel then the order gave to halt awhile at Siah.

This place it is a lovely spot, in the centre of a valley,
    Upon the side of a running stream, where balmy breezes dally.
Here we stayed to rest ourselves and get something to eat,
    And from the brook quench our thirst, with water pure and sweet.

And when we had refreshed ourselves, we once more took the road,
    And down the hills for many a mile, we onward gaily strode.
We branched off down a narrow path, to the village of Kalsie,
    The Band it played, which seemed to fill the natives all with glee.
'Tis seldom that they hear the sound of music soft and sweet,
    And when they do, it is by them regarded as a treat.

Although 'twas cool up in the hills, as lower down we got,
    The sun shone fiercer until the day became quite hot.
Our clothes were wet with honest sweat, and blistered were our feet,
    And as we marched along that day we suffered from the heat.

At length the camp ground we did spy, which was a welcome sight:
    We soon got there, pitched our tents, and turned in for the night,
And who can doubt but we then slept the deep sleep of the just,
    For 27 long miles we'd marched amidst the heat and dust.
And when we come to look it o'er, and back the march to scan,
    We cannot help but think it was a credit to each man.

Next morning was the ninteenth, but we did not march away,
    Our Colonel gave an order that we'd halt there for the day.
Our camp was pitched upon a piece of splendid level ground,
    In front of which there ran a stream where silvery fish abound.
And in our rear, not far away, there stood a forest drear,
    Where lived the howling jackal and the nimblefooted deer.

And, as the time it was our own to use as we thought best,
    Some of our men they passed the day in camp with song and jest,
And some they went across stream to climb the hills and crags,
    Whilst others to the forest went to chase the noble stags.

As for myself I went to look at Alexander's stone,
    Which o'er two thousand years has stood in solitude alone.
Upon whose side there is inscribed a part of history's page,
    An interesting relic of a dark and bygone age.

This relic is a treaty, which is here to be seen,
  And which a many years ago was concluded between
The powerful Rajah Porus, who was a native King,
  And the mighty Alexander, whose praises poets sing.

Tho' both these great men from earth have long since passed away,
  The stone and treaty still remain, and will for many a day.
And as I wandered back to camp, I murmered whilst alone,
  May all our honors last as long as Alexander's stone.

Next morning early we did start upon our way again,
  And every man was blythe and gay, and free from care and pain.
We shortly crossed a large bridge, by the bright light of the moon,
  Which brought us to that fertile spot, the valley of the Doon.
And as daylight appeared, through a soft and misty haze,
  A splendid scene was brought to view to our delighted gaze.

This valley is a lovely spot, and nicely situated :
  Its soil is rich, and also is most highly cultivated.
Here the tea plant is laid out for miles in long straight rows,
  And wheat, tobacco, and Indian corn in rich abundance grows.

We halted here to rest awhile, in this most charming place,
  And when we had once more fell in, we journeyed on apace.
And as we passed plantations of the snow white cotton tree,
  I thought the people of the vale ought to contented be.

We jogged along until we'd gone about ten miles or more,
  The word to halt was given at a place called Futtehpore.
And here we quickly pitched our camp, on ground just by the road,
  Not very far away from where a sparkling river flowed.
Upon whose sides abundance grew of green-leaved watercress,
  Which could be had by those who liked to pluck it for their mess.

Next morning off we went again, before the break of day,
  And by the time the sun was up, was well upon our way.
The crisp and healthy morning air it filled our hearts with joy,
  The milestones they seemed closer as we briskly passed them by.

And as we marched, the Band they played a quick and lively tune,
  And very soon we left behind the valley of the Doon.
We passed into another range of wild and lofty hills,
  Down whose sides, spring water ran in bright and silvery rills.
For several miles the road was lined with large and stately trees,
  And from the mountain tops there blew a soft refreshing breeze.

Upon a small hill near the road, a tribe of monkeys sat,
    Whose occupation seemed to be to quarrel and to squat.
And as we passed they one and all began to grin and gabber,
    To fight and bite, and clamour too, also to screech and jabber.

It seemed like bedlam upside down, 'twas such an awful clatter,
    As in the monkey language they at us began to chatter.
Now, what the monkey language is, I'll tell you if you wish :
    It is a mixture of Parsee, Pushto and crab English.

Some of these monkeys seemed to say, as they their nuts did gabble,
    Hallo, fifth, now give it 'em hot, when you get up to Cabul.
Of course we did not need to be reminded what to do,
    Especially by a crowd of such inferior beings too.
Our superiority just to show, we not a word did say,
    But treating them with cold contempt, continued on our way.

When we'd been marching for a while, to music's cheerful strains,
    We altogether left the hills, and entered India's plains.
And soon we came to Badshahbagh, which ended this day's tramp,
    We halted, piled our arms, and then we quickly pitched our camp.

While we were here, our Colonel gave an order out that we
    Would get a suit of white clothes dyed, a colour called khakie.
This khakie is a dusty brown, a good colour but plain,
    'Tis worn by all our troops when they take part in a campaign.

Although it don't improve a man, nor yet make him look pert,
    'Tis much preferred to red or white, it does not show the dirt.
And being the colour of the ground, it fills our foes with fear,
    Because they cannot see our men until they are quite near.

We struck our camp and started off at four o'clock next morn,
    Just as the stars began to fade, and day began to dawn.
The road we took in gallant style, and jogged along quite smirk,
    We looked a regiment that was fit for rough and ready work.

The natives from each village came to look and to admire,
    Until at length we halted at the camp ground of Kalsiah.
We piled our arms and pitched our camp, and quickly settled down,
    Our stomachs filled, some of us went to look around the town.

Alas there was no town to see, which filled us with disgust,
    Nought but a village, that was filled with heaps of filth and dust.
And as this very ancient place did not smell very sweet,
    We quickly beat what soldiers call, an honorable retreat.

Not very far away from camp, a large canal ran by,
  'Tis used for irrigation when the weather's hot and dry.
And when the evening it got cool, and day was growing dim,
  Most of our men refreshed themselves by going there to swim.

Next morning it passed much the same as mornings gone before,
  We struck our camp and started off towards Saharunpore.
For several miles our route it lay by fields of growing grain,
  When these were passed we entered on uncultivated plain.
This plain looked very bleak and wild, and also very bare,
  With nothing but a few trees and a mud hut here and there.

We suffered much from heat and dust, the march was long and trying,
  But still we jogged on cheerfully, downheartedness defying.
Until at last Saharunpore came gradually in view,
  Which looked a noble city as we nearer to it drew.

We passed in at the city gate, marched through the main bazaars,
  Where groups of natives stood, and stared at us bold sons of wars.
The streets, they were so crowded with the Moslem and Hindu,
  It was with some difficulty we managed to get through.

When we had reached the other side, and passed the last bazaar,
  We marched out by another gate, but had not to go far.
We halted near a tope of trees, which was our destination,
  Half way between the city and the local railway station.

Saharanpore city is as yet the largest we've passed through,
  On this account I now will try it to describe to you.
It has some very fine bazaars and leading thoroughfares,
  Where cunning native merchants sit amidst goods and wares.
Its streets are constantly filled with a large and motley crowd,
  Who seem to have nothing to do but smoke and talk aloud.

It also has a splendid mosque, which all good moslems love,
  Whose lofty spires seem to touch the bright blue sky above.
The followers of Mahomet, they come here five times a day,
  To Allah and the Prophet then, they most devoutly pray.
And all over this large city Hindoo temples do abound,
  Where poor unenlightened heathens are always to be found.

A large botanical garden lies just outside the city,
  And from its looks it seems to be as useful as its pretty.
Tis just the place where one could spend many pleasant hours,
  For here are grown most every kind of sweetly scented flowers.
This garden is looked after at the Government expense,
  Who do not from the city get the slightest recompense.

When we take it altogether, I think Saharunpore
  Is very much more favoured than most native cities are.
Ther seems a wealthy look about its street of shops and stalls,
  Although grim poverty is not unknown within its walls.

About this interesting place I have no more to say.
  I'll tell you how by us in camp the day was passed away :
When we were nicely settled down upon our camping ground,
  Some very curious characters began to gather round.

And as the afternoon wore on, the camp they did invade,
  Some of them to amuse us came, and others came to trade.
But still they one and all had got the same object in view,
  Which was to make as many pice as ever they could do.
As every man somehow must live, these people we can't blame,
  Had we to scratch along like them of course we'd do the same.

There were some ragged mendicants, and curious old fiddlers,
  Some pedlars and a couple of native Jeremy Diddlers.
Besides the wondrous dancing dog, and living skeleton,
  We also had a counterfeit Professor Anderson.
Who made an empty box seem full with one wave of his wand,
  And did some other clever tricks by simple sleight of hand.

Next came some Indian jugglers, and a man who swallowed fire,
  Also a clever monkey who did Blondin on a wire.
There also was an acrobat who threw himself about,
  And sometimes seemed as if he would himself turn inside out.
Same opium eating snakecharmers, and nautch-wallahs also,
  The only thing deficient was the bones and old banjo.

Whilst watching these performances, the time went quickly by,
  And I must say that we enjoyed ourselves right merrily.
And when the night was drawing near these people went away,
  And seemed contented with the pice they'd got from us that day.

At ten o'clock next morning we struck camp once again,
  And neatly packing all our tents we took them to the train.
And in the luggage vans we then stowed everything away,
  In doing this we occupied the best part of the day.

When all our things were cleared away, the "fall in" it did sound,
  And to the music of the Band we left the camping ground.
Then to the station we did march in all our martial pride,
  And as the train was waiting there, we quickly got inside.

Before we'd time to settle down our men began to mumble,
  The way that we were packed would cause a saint to grumble,
The carriages we occupied were badly crushed and bruised,
  By the lowest class of natives they had many years been used.

And from their nasty dirty state the smell was very strong,
  To put us in such carriages I'm sure was very wrong.
Each compartment was divided by upright iron bars,
  Each seat was nothing but a plank, all over cuts and scars.

How we were treated I am sure our Colonel did not know,
  They herded us together, just like wild beasts in a show.
But as we knew that grumbling would not do the slightest good,
  Like sensible men we settled down, and did the best we could.

Just as the station clock struck six a shrill whistle did blow,
  Which was the signal for the train upon its way to go.
The iron horse then gave a screach, and did no longer stay,
  And bidding Saharunpore farewell, we started on our way.

Across the plain our train sped on, like some wild fiery steed,
  For several miles we went along, at almost lightning speed.
Although at this high rate of speed for long we did not go,
  The rate that we then travelled at was far from being slow.
And as the train it goes along, I think that I will try
  To give a slight description of the places we passed by.

The first place of importance that we came to on our way,
  Was the station of Umballa, where a short time we did stay.
Here we managed for to get some biscuits and some beer,
  The railway folks did not forget to charge us pretty dear.

For well they knew a soldier will, if he has got the pice,
  Have what he wants, and this is why they charged us such a price,
Go where you will 'tis much the same all over Hindustan,
  They from the British soldier get as much as e'er they can.
As I speak from experience, I know you will not doubt it,
  But as it cannot altered be, I'll say no more about it.

Umballa is as healthy a spot as any to be found
  Upon the plains of India for many miles around.
The barracks here are nicely built, in large and handsome groups,
  Sufficient to accommodate two thousand British troops.

The great Durbar of sixty-nine was celebrated here,
  Between the late Lord Mayo and the then Afghan Ameer.
The way the Ameer was received was something very grand,
  The Viceroy heartily greeted him, and shook him by the hand.

He treated him with kindliness, and feasted him for days,
  And showed for him his great respect in many kinds of ways.
To some loyal Native Princes he introduced him then,
  And for him held a grand review of several thousand men.

A treaty it was then drawn up, and signed by Shere Ali,
  In which he vowed he'd always be our firm and faithful ally.
He said that to us he'd be true, and never break his word,
  Lord Mayo he then gave to him a diamond hilted sword.

Also a splendid portrait of Her Majesty the Queen,
  Set in a frame of stones so rare, as are but seldom seen.
He also got a battery of powerful Armstrong guns,
  And several thousand stands of arms, and presents for his sons.

But time has proved he played us false, and did not keep his word,
  Although he took good care to keep the portrait and the sword.
He did not scruple for to turn these Armstrong guns upon
  The very Government from whom he had received them from.
Which ought to be enough to show, that an Afghan alliance
  Is nothing but an empty farce, in which there's no reliance.

Time being up, we quickly took our places in the train,
  The whistle on the engine blew, and of we went again.
On on we went for hours, through the darkness of the night,
  Next morning still we journeyed on, till long after daylight.
For many hours in the train we'd travelled on our route,
  And felt so stiff and crampy that we wished that we were out.

We saw no place of note, until we passed Amritsur's walls,
  A place that's celebrated for its silk and Indian shawls.
It can boast of a splendid temple, where faithful Hindus go,
  And which was built by Ranjeet Singh, a long long time ago.
Two companies of Europeans are quartered in its Fort,
  To gain which, many years ago the British bravely fought.

At last, shortly before midday, we gave an hearty cheer,
  For, in the distance we could see the rest camp at Mean Meer.
These rest camps, they are pitched upon a piece of open ground,
  And near large railway stations they are mostly to be found.

When troops are travelling by rail, they rest here through the day,
  And then when night comes round again, they journey on their way.
They are put up in October and are taken down in May,
  And during the summer months are somewhere stowed away.

It was not very long before we to the station came,
  When, at the platform we had stopped, we quickly left the train.
Ourselves, we then shook out a bit to drive away the cramp,
  When all the regiment had fell in, we marched towards the camp.
Which was upon a sandy plain, a short distance away,
  And there we made ourselves at home and rested for the day.

And soon we got our breakfast, and our dinner both together,
  The meat we got it was so tough, I thought that it was leather.
But, as most of us were hungry, we did not care a jot,
  With knife in hand we set to work, and quickly eat the lot.
And when this operation had been cheerfully gone through,
  Our appetites were satisfied, and hunger from us flew.

Soon after this we got a pint of commissariat beer,
  For which each man he paid six pice, which was not very dear ;
And, as this beer was good, we thought the money well spent,
  To finish up the day, we had a concert in each tent.

What songs were sung in other tents, I'm sure I cannot say,
  But still I'll tell how in my own the time was passed away.
We had comic songs of every kind, and serious songs as well,
  And recitations old and new, including Little Nell.

We also had Round goes the Wheel, and Pity Poor Old Joe,
  Merrily goes the Mill my Boys, and Ring the Old Banjo.
The Minstrel Boy, the Anchor's weighed, when Paddy his pension,
  Sweet Evaline, and other songs too numerous to mention.
And I must say that all of these by us were much enjoyed,
  And so you see the way that we our leisure time employed.

But as everything must have an end, as life we journey through,
  Of course our concert was destined to have an ending too.
That we were sorry when it came, I can't help but confess,
  It was brought to an ending by the sounding of the " dress."
Which was the signal to prepare, to make a speedy flight,
  And in the train once more to pass, another wretched night.

We soon fell in, and then marched down to the railway station,
  And there we all were drawn up in the usual formation.
We got into the carriages just as the night before,
  When every one was settled down, we started off once more.
And once again we were packed in away, far from serene,
  A style that by a Frenchman would be called *a la sardine,*

The first place that we came to was the station of Lahore,
    The capital of the Punjab, and a city noted for
Its being a most extensive and populated place,
    Inhabited by the Sikhs, who are a tall and warlike race.

And as the evening wore along, we journeyed pretty fast,
    At length we came to Wuzeerabad, which place we quickly passed.
'Tis nicknamed little Sheffield, because there is here made
    A large amount of cutlery, which is its staple trade.

We travelled on throughout the night, past stations near a score,
    And over rivers large and small we crossed a dozen or more.
And in the morning at daylight, as in the train we sat,
    A mile or two in front we saw, the city of Gujrat.
We quickly to the station came, and stayed there for awhile,
    And then we journeyed on again for many a weary mile.

And when our journey's end drew near, our spirits they revived,
    And shortly after ten o'clock at Jhelum we arrived.
It was not very long before we all had left the train,
    And then we were fell in, and marched on to an open plain,
Which was to be our camping ground, our tents were to be here,
    And so of course we halted, piled our arms, and then stood clear.

And very shortly after this we fell in once again,
    And marched to unload the tents, and bring them from the train.
When this was done, and we had brought our baggage all away,
    We set to work and pitched our tents, and settled for the day.

Jhelum : it is a good sized place, and greatly noted for
    Its large stores of provisions, and its munitions of war.
From the lower parts of India, are brought here by the train,
    A large amount of warlike stores and many tons of grain.
Large quantities of transport by Government are hired,
    To take these stores to the front as often as required.

Just by the native city, the Jhelum river flows,
    The country round is very good, and corn in plenty grows.
Jhelum is the railway terminus, for here the line it ended,
    Although in course of time no doubt, it will be much extended.
On this account we knew full well that we would march from here,
    And this we could most cheerfully do without the slightest fear.

Next morning we stayed where we were, and did not march away,
    As all our transport was not there, we halted for the day.
Next day we made a proper start, in earnest we began,
    To jog along with might and main towards Afghanistan.

We marched along the Grand Trunk Road, a long road to be sure,
  Full eighteen hundred miles in length from Calcutta to Peshawar.
We journeyed on until we'd gone twelve miles upon our way,
  And then at Deena we did halt, and stayed there for the day.

Next morning we marched on again, some fourteen miles or more,
  We halted, piled our arms, and then our tents pitched at Sohawer.
This camp ground it was much cut up, and far from being good,
  'Twas inches thick with dust, but still we did the best we could.

We went upon our way next morn, and cheerfully each man
  Stepped boldly out until we came to camp Goojire Khan.
And here we quickly set to work, and pitched our tents upon
  Some ground, which was no better than the camp we'd come from.
Most all the camps were much cut up by regiments gone before,
  Who halted here when on their way, to take part in the war.

Again we started on our way, at five o'clock next morning,
  And manfully we took the road, just as the day was dawning.
And when at Mundra we arrived, we stopped there for the day,
  And then, when morning came again, continued on our way.

Before we had gone very far, we on our right espied
  A very large mausoleum, upon whose site there died
The famous horse Bucephalus (a theme of ancient lay),
  Who bore Great Alexander through many a deadly fray.

And by this mighty conquerer, this charger was adored,
  Who, when he knew the horse was dead, greatly his loss deplored.
He built this large mausoleum to show his great regret,
  Which o'er two thousand years has stood, and still is standing yet.

We travelled on, and in our rear soon left this relic rare,
  And on arriving at Rewat, we quickly settled there.
This place can boast a large bazaar, the scenery round is grand,
  Not very far away from camp, an ancient mosque does stand.
And which is said to have been built two thousand years since,
  To celebrate a victory by some great native prince.

And near this mosque are several tombs disfigured by decay,
  'Neath whose crumbling slabs tis said the bones of great men lay.
I tried to find out who they were, and when they were laid low,
  But, though I asked the natives there, I could not get to know.
I thought as I stood there, and gazed upon these ruins old,
  That had they the power of speech what tales they could unfold.

Next day we started off again, for Pindee we were bound :
  With hearts so light and gay as we stepped smartly o'er the ground.
For well we knew when we got there, ourselves we could enjoy,
  And anything that we might want at Pindee we could buy.

For many miles we travelled at a quick and regular pace,
  And in the course of time came to this large and handsome place.
We set to work, and soon did pitch our little canvas town,
  When this was done we one and all where quickly settled down.

This being the second of the month, it was the very day,
  That by the custom of our corps, we were to get our pay.
At two o'clock the pay was drawn, and was at once served out,
  Then most of us cleaned up and went to have a look about.

The order was each man would be in his serge clothing dressed,
  And thus decked out each one amused himself as he thought best.
Two other regiments near us lay, the twenty-fifth and twelfth,
  With these some of us fraternized, and drank each others health.
We wished Old England's foes ill-luck, and to our hearts content
  We sang and danced until tattoo, then back to camp we went.

Next day we halted where we were and nothing much occured,
  Those not on duty had the day to pass as they preferred.
And as the time it is my own, this station I will now
  Describe to you as well as my abilities will allow.

Rawal Pindee is a splendid place, its roads are fine and wide,
  And shaded by large spreading trees, which grow upon each side,
Handsome buildings in nice gardens, near these roads do lie,
  Mostly occupied by officers in Government employ.

There is one princely residence, I must not overlook,
  To live in which would not demean a marquis or a duke.
And here resides the officer commanding the division,
  Lieutenant General F. F. Maude, a man of firm decision.

It also has some large hotels, and storehouses for trade,
  Also a splendid piece of ground, on which the troops parade.
In time of peace four thousand men its garrison compose,
  The British part of these are housed in spacious bungalows.

The scenery round is quite as good as one could wish to see,
  Provisions are cheap, and can be had in any quantity.
Tis just the place f r a European to take up his abode,
  The station of Rawal Pindee is the finest on this road.
Its ancient native city is of enormous size,
  When by our army it was took, they got a goodly prize.

Next day we did not march away, but still in Pindee stayed,
  And as the day was Sunday, we attended church parade.
But when the following morning came, we packed up everything,
  And then we once more started off en route to Janee ka Singh.
And when at this place we arrived, we pitched our tents close by
  Where stood the only place of note, a very large serai.

Next morn our camp was all astir before the break of day,
  When the tents were struck and packed, we went upon our way.
Our march during the first three miles lay up a slight ascent,
  Upon a small hill near the top there stood a monument.
And just beneath a fountain stands alongside the road,
  From which a never-ending stream of sparkling water flowed.

The reason these memorials, this spot are raised upon,
  Is to commemorate the name of General Nicholson,
Who for Old England fought and bled, in many of her wars,
  And, like a true born Englishman, died in his country's cause.

When these were pass'd we journey'd on with hearts and spirits light,
  And when two miles from camp we passed a large hill on our right.
Upon this hill there was a tomb, a structure good and sound,
  And which is seen for many miles. by all the country round.
Here Hussan Abdul lies at rest, a man of ancient fame,
  From whom, a many years ago, this valley took its name.

Leaving this ancient tomb in rear. we continued our tramp,
  And met the Band of the fifty-first, who played us into camp.
And here the pitching of the tents was very quickly done,
  And then we put ourselves to rights, and soon were all A1.

Hussan Abdul was a lovely place, long in the distant past,
  Though since then time's destroying hand has over it been cast.
History says it once could boast of gardens filled with flowers,
  Along whose splendid paths were built the most magnificent bowers.
Abundance of delicious fruits, grew on its groves of trees,
  Whose fragrance soothed the senses as it floated on the breeze.

Its marble basins, they were filled with gold and silver fish,
  And everything could here be had that any one could wish.
'Twas here the mighty Jehanguire spent many hours alone,
  Or with Sultana Nourmahal, he sometimes here would roam.

In later days sweet Lalla Rookh did grace its emerald sward,
  Accompanied by Feramorz, the young Cashmerian bard.
Who told to her his grand old tales, and romances of love,
  In tones so exquisite they seemed inspired from above.

Alas, this grandeur of the past has vanished from the scene,
  And of its bowers and fountains now hardly a trace is seen.
Where everything was lovliness, when seen by Lalla Rookh,
  There nothing now remains, except a few trees and a brook.

We left this most romantic spot, next morning about four,
  And took the road in gallant style, and marched to Lawrencepore
And there we made ourselves at home, like soldiers gay and free,
  And soon we were as comfortable as men in tents could be.
In company with other corps, in camp twelve days we stayed,
  The principal cause of this delay was to form a Brigade.

With Native troops our regiment was formed into due course,
  The 2nd Brigade, 2nd Division, Peshawer Valley Field Force.
Which was to be commanded by a most experienced man,
  Brigadier General Doran, a true born gentleman.

We were ordered to move upon November, the eighteenth day,
  And so we struck our camp and went once more upon our way.
The march this day was hot and long, the road was very dusty,
  Such exercise as this will keep a man from getting rusty.
At length at 10 o'clock a. m. at Attock we arrived,
  When each man to make himself snug had very soon contrived.

And, when the day was near its close and getting cool, I thought
  That I would then a visit pay to Attock's noble fort.
This fort is built upon a fine commanding piece of ground,
  I soon got there and then, of course, began to look around.

'Tis very well provided with all kinds of warlike stores,
  Which in enormous heaps are piled upon its ancient floors.
'Tis plain to see those solid walls were built in days of yore,
  Their strength is great, they yet will stand many long years more.

Its garrison is two companies of British infantry,
  Also a garrison battery of royal artillery.
Whose very powerful Armstrong guns, with barrels grooved and wide,
  In case of need could sweep the land for miles on every side.

Old as this noble fortress is, 'tis near as good as new,
  It still is firm, and easily could withstand a siege or two.
Should enemies in future days, to take this place combine,
  They'll find it can hold out almost for any length of time.

We journeyed on again next day as lighthearted as boys,
  And were some distance on our way before the sun did rise.
We quickly crossed o'er Attock bridge, which spans the Indus river,
  A sight of whose dark rushing waves will make a Hindoo shiver.

For, by his own religion he this river must not cross,
  By doing so his caste is broke, which is a fearful loss.
For sake of caste a Hindoo will go through all kinds of strife,
  He values it so much, it is as dear to him as life.

The treacherous Cabul river, a current dark and drear,
  Into the river Indus flows, a short distance from here.
By natives who dwell near its banks, 'tis looked upon with dread,
  For nought but whirlpools and quicksands compose its hateful bed.

But though these waters are despised, still in the bright sunshine
  The scenery round about this spot is something most sublime,
For on each side is seen a vast amount of growing grain,
  And villages surrounded by large fields of sugar-cane.

The trees and shrubs they glistened with the early morning dew,
  And as we marched along, we passed by many a lovely view.
At last Akora we did reach, which did not cause much sorrow,
  We halted, put up our tents, and stayed there till the morrow.

And, when next morning's light appeared, we started off again,
  With bold and manly step towards Nowshera's sandy plain.
And as the march was very short, we jogged along all right,
  And when we'd gone about nine miles, the station came in sight.

And as the buildings of the place in front of us did rise,
  We were met by the splendid band of the IXth Holy Boys,
Who played us to our journey's end, with marches three or four,
  And then we quickly settled as we had often done before.

The scenery about our camp was far from being grand,
  Hardly a thing was seen except a plain of burning sand,
Which seemed to be almost red hot, and as a consequence
  The heat here in the summer time is often most intense.

In fact this place is said to be, take it throughout the year,
  One of the hottest found upon the plains of India.
To those who form its garrison, the climate it is such,
  Do what they will they cannot help but feel it very much.

When we to this camp came we thought we would leave next day,
  But we were much mistaken, for twelve days we had to stay.
And as we were most anxious to get over the frontier,
  Of course we grumbled very much at having to stop here.

We wished to cross at once, and make the savage Afghans fly,
  Still for all that while we were here the time went quickly by,
In practising the new attack, and several other drills,
  And doing outpost duty on some low and sandy hills,

Nothing of note occurred till at twelve o'clock one day,
    An earthquake it surprised us as it passed along our way.
It caused our tents to rock about like vessels in a squall,
    And made the barracks totter so, I thought that they would fall.

It also made large trees to reel about most dreadfully,
    And caused the sand to roll along like waves upon the sea.
The natives were so frightened that they from their huts did run,
    Although the shock was most severe, no damage much was done.

But this was not the only thing that came and left its stamp,
    For soon a sandstorm then arose and swept right thro' our camp.
And with great clouds of sand and dust it filled the atmosphere,
    Which made most of us wish that we were miles away from here.

Sometimes these sandstorms are so dense as to obscure the light,
    And turn the middle of the day almost as dark as night.
And when they are accompanied by winds that are quite hot,
    It takes some time before they can be easily forgot.

Besides the earthquake and sandstorm, I don't much else remember,
    For nothing much took place until the second of December.
When suddenly an order came, which said our regiment would
    At once march forward to Peshawar as quickly as it could.

This order (which delighted us), came in the morning time,
    And so we struck our camp and was upon the road by nine.
And as we left Nowshera's plain, our hearts were light although
    Along a dusty road we had nigh thirty miles to go.

We travelled on for several hours beneath a scorching sun,
    Which made us sweat most freely, as it down upon us shone.
When fifteen miles had been traversed, which was about half way,
    We came to camp Taroo, and there about an hour did stay.

During which time we had a rest and got something to eat,
    We also got a pint of beer, which was a proper treat ;
As we were parched and thirsty, it was by most of us prized,
    And after all our journeying was not to be despised.

The hour it having passed away, we all fell in once more,
    And then we smartly marched along the valley of Peshawar.
O'er which sometimes foul cholera breathes forth its fatal breath,
    On this account by Europeans 'tis called the Valley of Death.

But of such fatal things as these we did not give a thought,
    But jogged along for miles until we reached Peshawar Fort,
Which soon was passed, and then as we the station nearer drew
    Nice gardens and fine bungalows came gradually in view.

From which a stream of people came with English faces fair,
  To have a look at us, and see what regiment we were.
But as it now was getting dusk, and night was drawing near,
  Our noble band of war dogs they could not see very clear.

What made it worse our features were almost as black as night,
  Caused by our being so long neath the sun's most powerful light.
Which had during our heavy march, throughout this weary day,
  Down on us bold Northumbrians shed many a fiery ray.

Our clothing and accoutrements were very thick with dust,
  Which covered every man just like a coat of dirty rust.
As thus all through the day had crept, and still o'er us did creep,
  We now looked very near as black as many a London sweep.

In fact a European said, in a tone of great surprise,
  Good gracious me it seems as if I can't believe my eyes.
Then walking nearer with a look of pure astonishment,
  Said he, I'm sure that this must be some Native regiment.

He'd hardly said the words, before each gallant Fusilier,
  Raised up his manly voice and gave a ringing British cheer.
Which to convince this dubious man, no doubt was quite enough,
  That we were not a native corps, but proper English stuff.

Soon after this another man, who looked both neat and trim,
  Came up to a Corporal and a question put to him.
His object was, he wanted to find out how many men
  Belonging to our regiment was marching with us then.

But it was asked in such a way, 'twas like an awkward pun,
  Which made the Corporal think that he would have a little fun.
" How strong is your regiment marching," the man said, by his side,
  " We are marching on as strong as bulls," the Corporal replied.

This did not satisfy the man, who gave a scowl, and then,
  " No, no," said he, " I want to know the number of your men."
" Oh ? very well," the Corporal said, "if you our clothing scan,"
  " You'll find the number five upon the shoulders of each man."

The man he frowned, then he said a few words which I'll mention,
  You fifth may be good fighting men, but have no comprehension.
But this outburst it only caused the Corporal to laugh,
  Which made the man quickly retire, he did'nt like such chaff.

Just at this time the bandsmen, they struck up a lively strain,
  Whose loud and cheerful tones made the place resound again.
Though well nigh wearied out these men, to give them all their due,
  They with great dash and spirit played as well as men could do.

When they were done the drums and fifes a merry tune began,
  Whose sprightly music seemed to put new life into each man.
And what with this and ringing cheers, our martial pride was fired,
  We felt just then that we could march much further if required.
And so we went along until the old barracks drew near,
  And halting on the parade ground, our journey ended here.

And such a journey as this was, is not so often done,
  For midst the heat and dust this day, nigh thirty miles we'd come.
And when it is considered the weight each man did bear,
  I think this hard day's marching was a credit to all there.
In addition to our folded coats, we also had besides
  Our rifles on our shoulders and our bayonets by our sides.

And seventy rounds of ball a man, water bottle and haversack
  Made up a load which was no joke, upon each soldier's back
Especially on a day like this, beneath an Indian sun,
  And I am sure no one could help but say it was well done.
The men who fell out on the road, in numbers were but few,
  Which showed when called upon what British troops can do.

The barracks not being occupied, our Colonel thought we might,
  To save the trouble of pitching tents, remain there for the night.
So he ordered us by companies, to march from where we stood,
  Into the barracks where each man took any place he could.

Some on boxes made their beds, and some upon the floor,
  Some on the tables or the forms, and some outside the door.
But we were not particular, to us it mattered not,
  So long as we had room to sleep, we didn't care a jot.

And now we had some supper and a pint of beer as well,
  Which was enjoyed right merrily, as many a man could tell.
And then we to our blankets went, and taking off our clothes
  Each man he then turned in and got a well earned night's repose

In order to give a better account of what the Fusiliers did on their arrival in Peshawar, I will discontinue writing in verse, and will continue my story in prose, as I think by writing in this manner I shall be able to give a much better description of what the regiment went through than I could by continuing the verses ; another reason for my doing so, is that I wish to introduce several pieces of poetry which were composed by some of my comrades.

After a good night's rest we got up next morning, December 3rd, greatly refreshed and quite fit for another hard day's marching should it be required. Most of us were up pretty early, and as we had nothing much to do till 10 o'clock (when there was to be medical inspection for a portion of the regiment), some of us thought we would go for a walk round the station in broad daylight, and see what kind of a place Peshawar was, as we did not get a proper view of it during our march through the evening before. So we started off at once, and during our ramble we passed along splendid roads lined on each side by edges of rose trees, alongside of which, about twenty feet apart, were planted some very large mulberry trees. Some of the bungalows were like little palaces, and the gardens in front and around them were something beautiful. In fact, that portion of Peshawar which is occupied by Europeans is just like a small paradise. In the native part of the station there are some very large bazars, where almost anything can be bought. There is also a very large native city, which is without exception inhabited by the most ruffianly set of people to be found in India. The majority of them are nothing but robbers, and a many of them are tribesmen who have committed murder in the neighbouring hills and have taken refuge here to escape the vengeance of the relatives of their victims. The number of persons killed by violence in this city, during the last twenty years, is said to be something enormous; even at the present time murders are almost of daily occurrence, and as a consequence there is plenty of work for the hangman. In fact throughout the

whole of the British empire there is not another city that
can be compared (for everything that is bad) to the native .
city of Peshawar. Should a European wish to enter it, he
must come provided with a pass, signed by most of the
head military men of the station. On his presenting this
pass at the main gate, several armed policemen are told off
to escort him around, as it would be almost certain death
if he attempted to go by himself. My comrades and
myself not being provided with a pass, of course we did not
go inside, but went a little further down and had a good
look at the fort. This fort is very large, and also a very
strongly built one. Besides being a defence for the country
around it also serves as an arsenal, being full of all kinds
of warlike stores for the use of the Forces on the frontier.
It is provided with several very powerful guns, some of
which are always pointing into the native city. This is a
very good precaution, as the people are liable to give trouble
at any time. On our way back we visited the cemetarys, in
which I am sorry to say some thousands of Old England's
sons are laid low. The gravestones, tombstones, and monuments tell a sorry tale. The names upon them are not like
they are on the same at home, in ones and twos, but are
here in scores and hundreds, and on some of the larger
monuments are engraved the names of nearly half a regiment, who have been taken away in a short time by either
cholera or fever. At times cholera is very prevalent in
this station, and when it once takes hold of a person it is
almost certain to end in death, as very few ever get over it.
There is also another disease which is much dreaded by
the people of Peshawar, which is called Peshawar fever: it is
a very sickly complaint, and seems to eat into the very marrow
of those who are unfortunate enough to be attacked by it, as
it is often felt by people years after they have left Peshawar.
The European troops that we saw, and who had been
stationed here during the previous summer, had a very pale
death-like of look about their features, which some of
them assured us would take some time to get rid of. Take

Peshawar station altogether it is a beautiful place to look at, but at the same time it is a place where no European will stay one minute longer than he can help. Having returned to the barracks we got our breakfasts, and soon after this the "fall in" sounded for the men who were to be medically inspected, which consisted of "I" and "E" Companies, made up to two hundred strong by "I" Company. After the inspection was over they were ordered to pack up their kits, load their tents on the camels, and march to Jumrood. At about midday everything being ready they started on their way. The road they took after leaving Peshawar was an extremely bad one, being six or eight inches thick with fine dust, which as they marched along, rose up in clouds around them and caused any amount of coughing and sneezing, which was not enjoyed very much. After they had gone about four miles they came to Hurri Singh ka Boorjh, which was our extreme frontier station ; there was nothing much to be seen here, except a few mud huts and a small fort, which was occupied by a number of armed police. Passing Hurri Singh our men entered Afghan territory, and as they did so they gave a ringing cheer, and marched on with might and main towards Jumrood Fort. The road, after leaving Hurri Singh, is exceedingly dreary, no trees, no villages, and no cultivation ; nothing but stones to be seen on either side, except the rotting carcass of some unfortunate bullock or camel lying here and there. On arriving at Jumrood the detachment marched straight into the fort (which at this time though large, was nothing but an old tumble down looking place, built of mud and stones) ; having halted, our men had to wait here a short time, while the Officer in Command (Major Creagh) made enquiries as to where they were to pitch their camp ; he having got the necessary information they were marched on to a very stony piece of ground, and put up their tents alongside of a company of the 17th regiment, who gave our men all the possible assistance they could, and also provided them with some good tea, which was very acceptable after the dusty march. It

was now about 6 p. m., the necessary pickets were thrown
out, and the remainder of the men then turned in for a
good night's rest. And now I think we had better leave
them and return to Peshawar, and see what the head-
quarters of the regiment have been doing in the meantime.
After the detachment had left at midday, an order was given
for the remaining portion of the regiment to pack all
their baggage and start for Hurri Singh at 2 o'clock. All
the transport animals having been loaded and 2 o'clock
having arrived, they fell in, and at once commenced their
journey, marching along the same dusty road as the detachment had taken before them. Having arrived at Hurri
Singh, they pitched their tents on the British side of the
frontier. When everything was in its place, and all the
guards had mounted, the rest of the men turned in and
settled for the evening.

As the head-quarters are likely to remain at Hurri Singh
for several days, I think we had better return to Jumrood
and follow the adventures of the detachment. On the
morning following their arrival, one hundred men of the
5th, with about the same number of Native infantry, were
ordered to proceed up the Khyber Pass, for the purpose of
escorting back to Jumrood a number of guns which had
been captured at Ali Musjid a short time previously by the
first division, under the command of General Sir Samuel
Brown. Falling in about 8 a. m., they commenced their
journey. The road, after passing Jumrood Fort, winds
through a country of stones, nothing but stones to be seen
on either hand, except a few graves here and there. After
going about three miles along this road our men suddenly
descended into the stony bed of a dried up river, and following this for about half-a-mile, they came to the mouth
of the renowned Khyber Pass, of which almost every one
has heard. The entrance to the pass lies between two large
hills, the one on the right has no particular name that I
know of, but the one on the left is called Shaghai Hill, on
the top of which we have already got a Signaling Station,

which is protected by a strong guard, composed of both
Europeans and Natives, and where the heliograph and
limelight are hard at work, day and night, flashing messages
to and fro, between Jumrood and Ali Musjid; after entering
the Pass, the road still winds along the dried up river bed,
and on every side, look where you will, there is nothing to
be seen but the bare rocky hills, no grass, no cattle, no
villages, nothing but barren ruggedness. When about two
miles have been traversed, the road commences to ascend
up the side of a hill on the left. This part of the road is
called Mackeson's road, and when our men had gone about
half-a-mile up it, they met the party from Ali Musjid (which
consisted of a large number of the 81st regiment) who were
bringing down the captured guns. Having halted, all the
guns, together with the necessary papers, were handed over
to the officer in command of the Jumrood party. When
this was done, the men from Ali Musjid commenced their
return journey, but hardly had they turned to the right about
when, pop, pop, went several shots from a low hill on the
right, which was speedily answered by rifles of the 81st,
whose steady fire, if it did the enemy no harm, it at least
caused him cease annoying us any more. The firing having
come to an end, so many of our men were told off to escort
each gun, and at once commenced their journey back to
Jumrood. The captured guns were 24 in number, of different
sizes and calibre; some of them were bronze six and nine-
pounders, the others were made of iron, and varied in size,
from the ordinary six-pounder mountain gun, to a twelve-
pounder field gun. The majority of them were mounted on
proper gun carriages with limber and everything complete,
and I believe were of European manufacture, as they seemed
to be too well finished to be of Afghan make; the guns and
their escort having reached the mouth of the Pass without
any mishap, they there met another party of the 5th, consisting of 1 Serjeant, 1 Corporal, 14 Privates, who were on their
way to relieve a party of the 81st at the Signaling Station on
Shaghai Hill; on arriving at Jumrood, the guns were made

over to the Ordnance Department, and our men were then marched back to their own camp and dismissed. Next day, December 5th, those men not on duty were up and hard at work by daybreak, clearing away the thousands of large and small stones, which were upon their camp ground, they had a heavy task before them, but as they worked with a will, by the time the breakfast bugle sounded at a quarter to eight, they had the whole of the front of the camp cleared, and a small wall made, 3 feet high, and about 50 feet long, which they had built alongside the road, with the gathered stones. It is really surprising to see the millions of stones that lie in and around Jumrood, one cannot help but wonder how they came there. I have heard that once upon a time it rained cats and dogs, and on another occasion, pitchforks ; but I think that some time or other there must have been a down right heavy shower of stones in this part of the world, as I cannot imagine how they could have come there in any other manner, unless, like Topsy, I s'pose dey grow'd. About 8 o'clock an order came for 50 of our men to fall in at once, and along with one hundred of the Mhairwarri Battalion, escort a large convoy of provisions, to Ali Musjid, returning to Jumrood the next day ; and as they are going upon a longer journey than the hundred men went yesterday, I think we had better accompany them, as it will give us an opportunity of seeing what kind of a place the Khyber Pass is, above Mackeson's road. The men having fell in, they then marched to the fort, where the convoy was loaded, and as soon as everything was ready, they started off, leaving ten men of the 5th, and ten men of the Mhairwarri Battalion, to form the rear guard, when all the convoy should have passed. On entering the Pass, the majority of the escort were thrown out to the right and left ; half-a-dozen of the Mhairwarris on one hill, and three or four Europeans on another, all the way along until the whole of them had been distributed, with the exception of ten Mhairwarris and ten of our men, who still marched in front of the convoy and formed the advanced guard. As the end of the convoy

passed each of the small parties upon the hill sides, they
descended into the Pass, and fell in with the rear guard.
The above is a very necessary precaution, as a convoy is
always liable to be attacked by the numerous budmashes
who prowl about the Pass. I will now continue to describe the
Pass beyond Mackeson's road. After passing the spot where
the captured guns were handed over to our men yesterday,
the road still continues to ascend gradually for about two
miles, when it crosses a range of hills, called Shaghai
heights; on the top of these heights there is a good sized
plateau, upon which the 81st regiment, several troops of
Bengal lancers, and a mountain battery are encamped;
passing Shaghai, the road suddenly descends into a wild
gorge, with a large mountain stream (called the river Jum)
rushing over its rocky bed, on the left of the stream was a
small mud fort, with a few trees, and some tall grass growing near it, and as there was nothing to be seen as far as
the eye could reach, but stones, rocks, and barren hills, this
place was indeed a real oasis in the desert. As the road
comes to an end just here, our men were compelled to wade
through the stream, up to their knees in water, which they
did for about 300 yards, when they came to Ali Musjid,
where the convoy was handed over to the commissariat,
and our men were ordered to remain till next morning
with the 51st regiment, who, along with some native troops,
were encamped on the right side of the stream. The
piece of ground on which this camp is pitched is completely
surrounded by hills, and upon one of them on the other
side of the stream, stands the celebrated fort of Ali Musjid,
which is much the same now as when it was taken a fortnight ago. It is garrisoned at present by a number of Native
infantry, and looks like a place that has been very roughly
handled. Here and there the walls are very much battered,
which was done by the shells from our forty-pounders. The
ground inside the fort is covered with rubbish and debris
of every description. Gunpowder, fuzes, pieces of clothing,
shot and shell, papers, harness, bullets, wheels, pieces of

gun carraiges, and many other things, were all mixed up in utter confusion. If this fort was thoroughly repaired, and armed with powerful guns, and strong breastworks for Infantry were thrown up on the surrounding hills, and the whole held by British troops, the position would be absolutely impregnable, and could not be taken by force, by the finest troops the world could produce. Early next morning our men began their return journey to Jumrood, escorting back an empty convoy, which consisted of a string of camels nearly two miles in length ; and as they passed down Mackeson's road, many of them were struck with the wildness of the scenery around them, and well they may be, for in the soft morning light the hills looked extremely weird and picturesque. These wild mountain ranges which run for miles on either side of the Pass, have given to the world a race of the wildest looking creatures that tramp the earth. Savage in countenance, wild in appearance, ragged and dirty in dress, the Afridee Afghan is a true type of a lawless robber, which he is. The rocks and hills throughout the Pass are bored on all sides with caves, in which these ruffians are in the habit of waiting for unsuspecting travellers, whom they either treacherously shoot down as they pass by, or else spring down on them, with their long knives, like lions upon their prey ; in either case it goes hard with their victims, who not only lose everything of value they may have about them, but in 19 cases out of 20 they lose their lives as well. On arriving at Jumrood, and the convoy having been handed over to the proper authorities, our men marched to their own camp where they were at once dismissed. On the following day, December 7th, another convoy was despatched to Ali Musjid, in charge of an escort, of the 5th and Mhairwarri Battallion, of the same strength as before, *viz.* 50 men of the 5th and one hundred Mhairwarris ; on their entering the Pass, the usual small parties mounted the hill sides, and all went well for sometime, when suddenly a volley was fired at a small party of the 5th (consisting of one Lance Corporal and five Privates) who were on the top of a hill about half way up Mackeson's road. Although none of our men were hit, the volley had been well aimed, as several bullets struck the rocks round about them. At the time the volley was fired our men were watching the Pass side of the hill, and the convoy passing beneath them, and consequently, although they knew well enough it came from the hills in their rear, they were not certain as to which of these hills it was, but getting well under cover, and loading their rifles they kept a good look out, and presently bang, went another volley from a hill a few hundred yards away, it had hardly been fired before our men sent a return volley clean into the same spot which had the effect of driving the enemy on to the peak of another hill. After a short time, another volley was fired by the enemy, and as speedily answered by our men as the volley that came before, and so it went on, volley for volley, our men always allowing the enemy to fire first, and then the next moment sending a well aimed volley right among them. After a while, a young officer of the Guides Cavalry (Lieutenant Hamilton, I believe it was) who was in charge of the convoy, came up with six more men of the 5th and about a dozen Mhairwarris, whom he ordered to commence firing, and the combined volleys of the whole party were so well aimed, that it drove the Afridees from rock to rock, and hill to hill. They seemed to be getting enough of it, for presently they came forward in force on the top of a hill, and after giving a loud yell and waving their tulwars and a black banner for a moment, they disappeared and were seen no more. This was the first encounter that any of the fifth had had with the Afghans, and though no one was hurt on our side, there were many narrow escapes, as the bullets of the enemy were flying around pretty close at times. Nothing more occurred, and the convoy arrived in safety at Ali Musjid, our men returning to Jumrood the next day. During the next few days, what with working round the camp, escorting convoys, and doing guards and pickets, the detachment had enough to do, and he was a lucky man who got every other night

in his blankets. On the 13th the head-quarters of the
regiment marched in from Hurri Singh, and pitched their
tents upon a large stony piece of ground. As the whole of
the regiment was now in Jumrood, the tents of the detachment was ordered to be struck, and pitched again in their
proper order, on the regimental camp ground, which was at
once done. Things went on much the same as before until
the morning of the 18th, when news was received that the
Guard at the Signalling Station on Shaghai hill, had been
attacked during the night. The particulars of which are as
follows: about the middle of the night the place was
attacked by a large number of Afridees, who fought so deter-
minedly that it took our men all their time to keep them back.
But British pluck and Martini rifles at length prevailed,
causing the enemy to take to their heels and run, *leaving
several* of their men on the ground.

As Private J. Ruddy has composed several verses upon
this affair, I think I cannot do better than bring them forward.

Come all you British soldiers, wherever you may be,
  I hope you'll pay attention, and listen unto me
While I relate the doings of this gallant little band,
  Who on that dreaded Shaghai ridge, so nobly took their stand.

On the eighteenth of December, the Afridees did attack,
  But like true British soldiers, we soon did drive them back.
Though our numbers were but few, not more than three score,
  To the hills we sent them flying, as we had done once before.

They thought to climb the mountains, and take us in the rear,
  While volley after volley, went whistling through the air.
But, steady lads, aim well and low, was whispered through our ranks,
  And quickly let these niggers see on us they'll play no pranks.

We soon found out the distance, and our rifles they did tell,
  That we would be victorious, by the numbers that had fell.
They very soon turned tail and run, while Allah was their cry,
  And down the hill pell mell we made these bold Afridees fly.

Led by Lieutenants Frend and Newton, two of Britain's sons,
  We every one stood to our post, and fired off our guns.
And by their good example, they showed their men the way,
  That Britons prove victorious amid the battle's fray.

Old England, she may well be proud of officers and men,
    When danger it brings to the front such brave heroes as them.
Always in camp or quarters they are frolicsome and gay,
    And in the hour of danger they are ready for the fray.

So now I'll wish success to all. that gallant little band,
    Who on that famous Shaghai ridge, so nobly took their stand.
They fought for England's glory, against her fiercest foe,
    Their deeds will sound victorious wherever they may go.

Shaghai hill had been attacked several times before the
occasion just narrated ; but the enemy had never given so
much trouble, nor fought so desperately as they did on the
present occasion, when they came in big force, and consequently got a big licking, which ought to be a warning to
them not to attack the hill again. A few hours after, after
the particulars of the above attack had been received, an
order was sent from the Brigade Office to our Colonel, saying
that 360 men of the 5th would be required to form part of
an expedition, which was to start from Jumrood next morning. Their destination being a place in the hills (on the left
of the Pass) called the Bazar Valley. The object of the
expedition was to punish a tribe of Afghans, called the Zukka
Kheyls, who were continually firing into all the British camps
along the Khyber line, and who had on one occasion attacked
a convoy near Lundi Khana, killing and wounding a number
of camel drivers, besides carrying off a large amount of stores.
Accordingly soon after 9 a.m. the following morning, December
19th, a force formed up near Jumrood Fort, which was composed as follows—3 guns on elephants of D.-A., Royal Horse
Artillery, 300 of the 5th Fusiliers, under Major Creagh, 60 men
(also of the 5th) under Captain Dyke, who were to act as a working party, being provided with powder, &c., for blowing up
purposes, 400 men of the Mhairwarri Battalion, and 50 Sabres
of the 13th Bengal Lancers. The whole force being commanded by Brigadier General Doran, c. b., who was accompanied by General Maude, and several of his Staff. At 10
o'clock the column moved of in the direction of the Pass,
which they entered. The march up Mackeson's road was

extremely slow, owing to the size of the force and to the road-way being blocked by the camels of two convoys, one going to Ali Musjid and the other returning to Jumrood. By the time Shaghai heights were reached it was nearly 3 o'clock. Here was left the elephants and the 3 guns of D.-A., Royal Horse Artillery, being joined in their stead by a mountain battery under Captain Broadfoot, R.-A. On leaving Shagha, the column marched on until within half-a-mile of Ali Musjid when it came to a halt on a piece of ground on the right side of the stream. It was now nearly 4 p. m., and as the force was going no further until darkness set in, our men had about two hours to themselves, during which time they got some hot tea, which was very acceptable as the day had been rather a cold one. About 6 o'clock the column fell in again, and after going a short distance along the stream they were ordered to cross, which they did wading through up to their knees. On reaching the other side they again halted, and were shortly afterwards joined by 200 men of the 51st regiment, under Lieutenant-Colonel Action, and 500 of the 2nd Goorkhas under Colonel Macintyre ; at about 7 p. m., darkness having set in, the troops began to ascend a large hill on the left, proceeding in the following order : 300, 2nd Goorkhas leading, accompanied by Captain Tucker, the Political Officer attached to the force, 3 guns Mountain Battery, 200 more of 2nd Goorkhas, the men of the 5th and 51st regiments, some cavalry, 3 more guns Mountain Battery, followed by the Mhairwarris and a few more cavalry who brought up the rear, as neither the Political Officer nor any other European knew anything about the country the column was to pass through, they had to depend for their information upon the Afghan guides who accompanied the force. The difficulties of the road had been greatly underrated, especially at night, as the eye sketch of the country taken at Ali Musjid, turned out to be quite useless, as will be seen further on. As the expedition was intended to be a sur-prise, strict orders were given, before leaving Ali Musjid, hat no one was to speak above a whisper, and on no account was any matches to be struck. On the column reaching the top of the hill just mentioned, they proceeded along a small and very winding path, this path being very narrow and the night extremely dark, the men were compelled to march in single file, each man keeping very close to the one in front of him, for fear of losing his road, as nothing could be distinguished two yards away. In this manner they proceeded across the tops of the mountains, until 3 o'clock next morning, when they descended into the bed of a river, on the side of which stood a village called Chora. Our men now thought they had reached their destination, and that the fighting part of the business was about to commence, especially when the guns in rear were ordered to be brought to the front, but they were greatly mistaken as they soon found out. The guides with the force (who seemed to have a very poor idea of distance) had told the Political Officer before starting, that the villages of the Zukka Kheyls could be reached by daybreak, but this was now found to be a great mistake, as the Bazar Valley was still miles away. All hopes of taking the enemy by surprise now being over, the column was ordered to halt till day light so as to allow the baggage animals in rear to come up. When they arrived, it was found that six mules carrying blankets belonging to the 5th Fusiliers were missing, and what made it worse no one seemed to know whether they had strayed away in the darkness, or had been looted by the numerous robbers who infest these hills. As the force were likely to be out for several days, and the weather in these latitudes being extremely cold, this was a great loss to those of our men to whom they belonged, but as they were gone, of course there was nothing left but to make the best of a bad job. About 7 o'clock the order was given for the column to advance, and the march forward was at once commenced. Passing the village, they followed the bed of the river for several hours. On all sides nothing was to be seen but steep hills with caves cut in the sides, similar to those in the Khyber Pass. The marching was very heavy, for besides the river bed being covered with stones of all sizes, a stream between 2 and 3 feet deep ran along in a zigzag fashion, which had during the day to be crossed some eighteen or twenty times. At length after repeated halts, to admit of the country ahead being reconnoitred by cavalry, an open plateau was reached about 3 p. m., at the southern end of which stood a village named Wallai (which, according to the programme, should have been reached long before daybreak). This village was found to be deserted, everything having been taken away, except a small quantity of grain (which was given to the mules) and a large pile of wood which came in very handy afterwards. The force was now within 4 or 5 miles of the Zukka Kheyls' main stronghold, and although the ground was rough we could have reached it easily in less than two hours, but for some reason unknown to me (unless it was that the men were tired, having been under arms since 9 a. m. the previous morning) they were ordered to halt where they were, and bivouac for the night. The guards having mounted, our men at once settled down and made themselves at home. The pile of wood having been brought over, the native cooks in a short time had several large *dixeys* steaming and singing away right merrily. These *dixeys* were filled with potatoes and meat, which, when cooked and served out to the gallant Fusiliers, was done full justice to, I can assure you. As night was now beginning to draw near, a number of strong pickets were posted on the neighbouring hills, each man (or rather those who had them) taking his two blankets with him; as darkness came on it began to get extremely cold, a heavy frost having set in, and by 8 o'clock the weather was so severe, that the water in the *dixeys* was frozen to solid ice. The order was now given for all the camp fires to be extinguished and the men to lay down for the night, and now began the troubles of those unfortunate men whose blankets were lost, even those who had them could hardly keep themselves warm, the cold was so intense; but those who had none, and especially the men on the hill tops, passed the night very miserably. When it is remembered there were no tents with the force, and that these men had been wading through water many times during the day, and that the only clothing they had on, besides their top coats, was their shirts and a thin suit of kirkie, it will at once be seen they were in a position not to be envied. Most of their comrades did what they could for them, either by lending them one of their own blankets (which could ill be spared) or by getting up in the night and letting their more unfortunate brothers lie down in their places a while; but for all this many a poor fellow lay shivering on the cold frozen ground for hours during this weary night, with nothing but the sky for a roof and a stone for a pillow. About 12 midnight an influential Zukka Kheyl, with an escort of several of his tribe, came to the camp and asked for terms: he was at once taken before Captain Tucker, the Political Officer, who after conversing with him for a short time, fined him (as the representative man of his tribe) the very moderate sum of one thousand rupees, and said it could either be paid in coin or cattle. The Zukka Kheyl objected to this on the plea that his tribe was too poor to raise so much; but said that both he and his people were willing to give up all the stolen properly that could be found in their villages—(very kind, wasn't it).

But this being far from pucca,
It did not suit Captain Tucker.
Who gave the wily Zukka
    At once to understand,

If to our terms he did not come,
We'd burn him out of house and home.
And drive him 'cross the hills to roam,
    With all his dastard band.

This made the cunning rogue look down,
And o'er his features spread a frown.
For well he knew he was done brown,
    And that he'd have to pay.

He got until next morn at nine,
To pay the thousand rupees fine.
Either in cattle or in coin,
    And then he went away.

9 o'clock having arrived, our terms not having been complied with, the troops were ordered to fall in and advance at once. As the enemy's villages were only a few miles away, and the column being almost sure to be back during the afternoon. The General gave orders for all the baggage animals to be left in Wallai, and a few men of each corps to remain behind to guard them. After the force had left the plateau they descended into the river bed, and following this up for about a mile they came to the entrance of the Bazar Valley, where in the distance about half way down, could be seen the villages of the Zakka Kheyls which were built near to the hills on the right. The column still continued to advance, until within half-a-mile of the nearest village, when the cavalry were ordered to approach as near as possible and reconnoitre, at the same time the 2nd Goorkhas were sent out to skirmish along the left of the valley, and the 5th Fusiliers were ordered to advance in skirmishing order straight towards the villages ; and as they started forward an Officer was heard to say to his men, " Now lads, we'll show them a trick or two directly ; " but this, also, was not to be, as they found out on reaching the villages, which were entirely deserted, and it could be plainly seen that the people had not long left, as some fires were still burning. The only things they seemed to have taken with them was their cattle. Each of the villages was provided with a large number of strong towers, more especially the principal one which was called Cheena, which when searched was found to contain a large store of walnuts (which somehow soon found their way into our men's haversacks), some hundreds of tons of grain, and a number of cocks and hens. These latter being the only enemies our men could find, they were at once attacked and then began a most desperate struggle, during which

there was any amount of skirmishing and hand to hand encounters; but British pluck at last prevailed and the Fusiliers were victorious. The enemy having been thoroughly beaten, they were all made prisoners, and, as after a short time some of them began to give trouble by attempting to escape from their captors, the whole of them were at once killed and their bodies reserved for the soup pot in the evening. In one of the villages a search party found two women and a decriped old man; the latter of whom was leisurely cooking some food over a small fire, and seemed greatly surprised when the Europeans entered his hut. On being brought before the Political Officer he innocently asked why we had come to Cheena, and Captain Tucker at once told him. These people were at once sent to the rear as the villages were about to be destroyed. The whole force having retired for some little distance, the working party of 60 men of the 5th Fusiliers, commanded by Captain Dyke, at once came to the front, and at once commenced burning the villages and blowing up the towers, under the direction of Captain Wright, R. E. The work of destruction lasted for several hours, during which time some prisoners were brought in by the cavalry, and a few heads of cattle was captured by detatched parties; but these when brought before the Political Officer, always turned out to belong to some friendly tribe. About 4 p. m. property valued at 5,000 rupees having been destroyed, and eleven large towers blown up, the troops were then ordered to return to Wallai, and on arriving there, they were very much surprised to find that during their absence, the party who had been left behind to guard the baggage had been engaged, and had captured some 200 head of cattle, and taken prisoners 70 or 80 women and a few old men and boys, besides having killed several of the enemy. The particulars of this little affair is as follows :—

Shortly after the force had left in the morning, one of our men saw a large party of men, women, and children, together with their cattle crossing the hills in the direction

of Wallai, thinking they were enemies, he at once informed
the officer of what he had seen, who got all the men together
that he could, and went out to meet them. On our men
getting near to them, they were saluted by a volley which was
at once returned, and after a short skirmish some of the
enemy having been knocked over, the remainder fled, leaving behind them their women and children, the old men and
boys, and the cattle, which was at once surrounded and
brought into Wallai, where they were when the column
returned from Bazar Valley. The whole of them were kept
in camp during the night (which passed much the same as
the night before), and were released early next morning by
order of the Political Officer. About 9 a. m. a very large
tower (in which during the night the General had slept)
was blown up ; and as the expeditionary force had now
completed the work for which they were sent out, they commenced the journey back again. Information was at this
time brought in by one of our Afghan spies, to the effect
that the missing mules, with the blankets of the 5th had not
strayed away in the darkness during the night march of the
19th, but had been looted by some marauders belonging
to a village called Burkas ; this village was situated on some
high ground, near the river bed, about a mile-and-a-half
from Wallai, and one company of the 5th Fusiliers and
one company of the Goorkhas, were at once sent on
in front with orders to burn it to the ground, which
they did,—rejoining the column some distance lower down.
All went well until about 11 o'clock, when, whilst the main
body of the force was marching through the narrowest
part of the defile, several shots were fired from the heights
on the right : the advanced guard of the 51st returned
the fire from the opposite heights, a company of the 5th
Fusiliers, and a small party of Mhairwarris, who happened to
be near, quickly ascended the heights, and joining the 51st,
the whole of them sent some tremendous volleys into the
enemy. This counter attack quickly succeeded in drawing
off the fire from the main column, and enabled it to pass

through, with the loss of only one man killed (a Goorkha) and one Mhairwarri, wounded. Wherever the shots of the enemy were fired from, a volley was immediately poured in from the opposite heights by our people, which nearly always caused them to leave their position and run along from rock to rock. Major Creagh, commanding the rear guard, consisting of two companies of the 5th, sent one company up the heights on the right side; and the enemy seeing their flank turned, quickly made off over the hills : the ground was very steep and pursuit would have been useless. Owing to the thick shrub that grew on the height it was impossible to calculate the actual loss inflicted ; but doubtless between 30 and 40 of them were knocked over, as many were seen to fall. The whole of the column having passed through, Major Creagh recalled the company of the 5th on the right, and also replaced the 51st men on the heights to the left, with another company of the 5th: this latter company along with a small detachment on the right remained in their position until the last of the column had got some distance ahead. A flanking party, cresting the hills to the left, were recalled by General Doran; and as the column had now traversed the most dangerous part of the defile, the whole of the men on the heights came down into the river bed, and continued their march, keeping a sharp look out to the right and left. On the column arriving at the village of Chora, they halted for a while to allow the men in rear to close up. In a short time the order was again given to advance, and the force then left the river bed and began to ascend a hill on the left, which brought them on to the same mountain path as they had traversed during the night march from Ali Musjid. A short distance along this path squatted about a dozen ruffianly looking Afghans armed to the teeth, who, on being questioned by the Political Officer, said they belonged to a neighbouring village, which at this time was friendly towards us ; this answer being deemed satisfactory they were allowed to remain where they were, but no sooner had our people passed them than they raised their jezails and fired a volley right among the rear guard (which showed how friendly they were), and the next moment began to scamper across the hills, followed by the fire of our men. A party would have been sent in pursuit, but for the General wanting to get the whole force into Ali Musjid before darkness set in, so for this reason these treacherous scoundrels were allowed to escape, no doubt to trouble our troops again some other day. After the firing had ceased, the column still continued its journey over the rough mountain tops (which even in the day time made marching very tedious), and arrived at the top of the hill overlooking the stream near Ali Musjid just before dark. At the bottom of this hill the 5th Fusiliers and Mhairwarris bivouaced for the night; the 51st, 2nd Goorkhas, and the Mountain Battery continuing the march to their respective camps, of Ali Musjid and Shaghai heights. Next morning the 5th and Mhairwarris left for Jumrood, escorting down the pass the elephants and guns of D.-A., Royal Horse Artillery, which had been left at Shaghai. On arriving there they each marched to their own camps, which every man was glad to reach after all the hard marching *and exposure* of the last few days. Politically the expedition is looked upon as a great success, as it has not only been the means of punishing a tribe of most lawless robbers, but it has enabled Mr. Scott, the Government Surveryor (who accompanied the force), to make a valuable survey of over eighty square miles of perfectly new country, where no *European* had ever been before.

On the evening of the 24th the following thanks were published in Brigade Orders :—

The Brigadier General desires to return thanks to all the Officers and men, composing the Forces which operated in the Bazar Valley during the late expedition, for the steadiness, endurance, and gallantry displayed by them during that operation.

The Brigadier General will not fail to bring to the notice of the Lieutenant General commanding, his high appreciation of the conduct of the entire force, more especially on the 22d instant, when they had to march and fight for hours without food.

Signed, &c. &c.

And this I think concludes all I have to say about the first expedition against the Zukka Kheyls.

During the next three or four weeks nothing very stiring occurred around Jumrood, but at the same time our men had plenty of work to do, for in addition to their ordinary duties of escorting convoys, doing guards and pickets, &c., every man that was available, was set to work repairing the road, between Jumrood fort and the Khyber Pass. For this a little extra pay was given, at the rate of one anna per hour. The weather during the above period was very cold indeed, especially at night when it was extremely so, and as might be expected this greatly effected the Native followers, many of whom died nightly. Every morning round about the camp, large fires were to be seen, each fire containing the body of some poor unfortunate Hindoo who had lately given up the ghost. This severe weather also told very much on the transport animals, especially the camels; who were dying in such large numbers, that several elephants were kept constantly at work, dragging the dead bodies to a piece of ground about half-a-mile away, where at one time the remains of nearly two thousand of these animals lay around. And so it went on from day to day. Our men were getting tired of Jumrood, and wanted to go further up the line of operations. It seemed to be very hard keeping such an old and well seasoned Regiment as the 5th in a place like this, doing some of the hardest work of the campaign, while other Regiments less seasoned and far younger in Indian service, were having it comparatively easier higher up. As all the regiments had given up all hope of leaving Jumrood until the termination of the war (when they would be sent back), they settled down and jogged along stolidly from day to day. About this time our gallant Drum Major composed a few

verses, which he entitled the "March to Cabul," and which
I cannot do better than at once bring forward :

October the eighteenth, day of tears,
Joy and gladness, hopes and fears.
The order was, the Fusiliers
    Would march that day for Cabul.

Along the road we made good speed,
Some hearts were gay, some dull indeed.
For why, all knew it was decreed,
    That we should go to Cabul.

Some left a happy home behind,
Others to care were almost blind ;
But all thought they would glory find,
    When they marched into Cabul.

We took the train at Saharanpore,
And sped through stations many a score.
Umballa, the Beas, and Phillor,
    Upon our way to Cabul.

At length we came to famed Mean Meer,
Where we got our dinner, and a pint of beer.
Then off to Jhelum we did steer,
    And thence to march to Cabul.

O'er hills and dales, and valleys too,
The old and bold, both brave and true,
Stepped smartly out, for well they knew,
    That they were bound for Cabul.

While on the road, both jest and song,
Kept hearts in time me marched along.
And who can say that we did wrong,
    In singing up to Cabul.

We stopped at Pindee, got our pay,
Enjoyed ourselves, then marched away.
At Lawrencepore we had to stay
    Before we got to Cabul.

Twelve days we stayed, then on again
To the front my lads, with might and main.
Alas Nowsher's sandy plain,
    Detained us yet from Cabul.

An earthquake came, it said begone,
A sandstorm too, it helped us on.
But we were ready, every one,
    For a glorious march to Cabul.

A long march too and no mistake,
Nigh thirty miles without a break.
But gaily we the road did take,
    For we were off to Cabul.

Peshawer was reached, a sickly place.
Then off again—a rattling pace.
But stopped once more within an ace.
    Of stepping into Cabul.

Twelve days we laid at Hurri Singh,
In hopes that fate at length would bring.
An order for us to have our fling,
    At the Ameer's troops in Cabul.

At last an order came quite swift,
That we to Jumrood Fort would shift.
Though but six miles, twas still a lift,
    Twas that much nearer Cabul.

Hard duty now, was all the cry,
To do their best, our men did try,
Where was the use of fighting shy,
    On the Frontier line of Cabul.

Hard work of all sorts was performed,
To do it every heart felt warmed,
But they would rather much have stormed,
    The stony walls of Cabul.

At Jumrood still we have a fear,
That Cabul's guns we'll ne'er,
Quo Fata Vocant give a cheer,
    Perhaps we'll yet see Cabul.

A word of praise to every one,
They well deserve it then I've done,
We'll never from the Afghans run,
    When we once get to Cabul.

Good luck attend each Fusilier,
And now I've done, but where's the beer,
Our Colonel, Boys, give him a cheer,
    We're ready now for Cabul.

Our late expedition to the Bazar Valley, although successful in severely punishing the Zukka Kheyls, does not seem to have been much of a lesson to them, as latterly they have been behaving as badly as ever, and have sworn to have revenge for the treatment they received a month ago. They are not satisfied with firing into our camps and convoys, and murdering our camp followers who incautiously stray away from their camps; but during the last week they have attacked several convoys, and on one occasion they actually managed to carry off no less than 75 camels, together with the stores they were carrying, so to punish them for committing these and other depredations, it has been decided to send another expedition against them, which is intended to act far more severely than did the last. On the evening of the 23rd of January an order was received stating that four companies of the 5th Fusiliers would be required to form part of the expeditionary force which was to leave Jumrood at 11 a. m., next day accordingly, when that time arrived, our right half battalion formed up near Jumrood Fort, along with the remainder of the force, which was composed as follows :—
2 guns on elephants of D. A., Royal Horse Artillery; 2 guns Mountain Battery; 4 companies, 25th Regiment; 4 companies, 24th Punjab Native Infantry, several troops of 13th Bengal Lancers; and a company of Madras Sappers and

Miners. Brigadier General Blythe having taken command, the column moved off in the direction of a pass about two miles to the left of the Khyber, and on arriving there, they journeyed through it for several miles. Like most of the Afghan passes the ground was very stony, it being a partially dried up river-bed intersected by a very winding stream, which had during the day to be waded through more than 40 different times, and as the water in some places was a good depth and at the same time very cold, of course this leg bath was not very enjoyable. The force continued marching until dusk, when it encamped on a piece of high ground on the right side of the stream. Although the troops had brought two tents per company, none of them could be pitched, as the ground was so thickly covered by trees and bushes. Strong pickets having been posted, the remainder of the men, after getting something to eat, rolled their blankets round them and turned in for the night, taking up their quarters on the cold ground ; and as the majority of them were still wet and the night a frosty one, of course they were far from being comfortable. Next morning about 7 o'clock, the force started off again, and after marching for 6 or 7 hours (during which time they cn'y went 4 or 5 miles, on account of the roughness of the road), they arrived at the village of Chora, where they were joined by a number of troops from Ali Musjid, which consisted of 200 men of the 51st Regiment, and about 300 each of the Mhairwarri Battalion, 45th Native Infantry, and the 2nd Goorkhas. Lieutenant General Maude having now taken supreme command, the force continued its march along the same route as that taken by the first expedition ; after going several miles, a halt was made at a place called Barakus on the right side of the stream, here the troops were ordered to bivouac (without tents) for the night. Camp fires having now been lit, those men not on guard or picket gathered round them, and made themselves comfortable. All went well for a time, when suddenly bang came a volley from the heights on the left, which was at once answered by the pickets ; this volley came right into the midst of a large fire (around which several men were sitting) and scattered it in all directions. The firing was kept up for about 2 hours, but happily the only damage done by the enemy was to kill a Captain's horse, and mortally wounded a baggage mule. As it was a very dark evening, it was thought useless to send any of the men to climb the hills, so some tremendous volleys were sent into the enemy's position, which eventually stopped his fire, and the remainder of the night pased quietly enough. On the following morning, January 26th, the force proceeded on its way along the river bed, and during the march was fired into several times from the different hills. During the afternoon the Bazar Valley was reached, it seemed to be entirely deserted, and not a sign of an enemy was to be seen anywhere; on arriving at Cheena the troops halted and pitched their tents. At dusk very strong pickets were posted all around the camp, and things went along all right until the men were getting their dinners, about 8 o'clock, when all at once a very heavy fire was opened on the camp from the hills on the right, which was answered by the pickets posted on high ground at the bottom. This firing was kept up for several hours, during which time we lost one man killed and one wounded, both being on picket at the time. Another man (a drummer) was shot in the back, whilst sitting down eating his dinner. Besides these casualties there were also very many narrow escapes, as the shots were flying about the camp in all directions; several passing through the tents over the head of the men inside. Early next morning a party was sent to scour the hills which were held by the enemy the night before; no enemy could be found as they had all made off before daylight, leaving their dead behind them. Seven bodies were found in a cave, besides several more, which were lying about on the hills, and which were quite numerous enough to show that the return fire of our men had not been wasted. About 8 a. m. a small column, made up from the 5th Fusiliers and 2nd Goorkhas, left the camp, and marched to the end of the Lundi Khana Valley, where communications were opened

with a force from Dhakka and Jellalabad, which was commanded by Brigadiers Tytler and Macpherson, and which
had been sent by General Sir Sam. Brown to co-operate with
General Maude. After signalling had been going on for
some time, the small column returned to camp (which during
their absence had been shifted into the centre of the valley)
shortly afterwards followed by the above force, which consisted of portions of the 4th Battalion, Rifle Brigade, 17th
Regiment, 6th Bengal Native Infantry, and the 4th Goorkhas,
and also 2 mountain guns. This reinforcement brought the
total number of fighting men up to 3,540. In the evening
strong pickets were again posted, and as soon as it got dark,
large parties of the enemy began to gather round the
camp yelling, Allah, Allah, and sending volleys in among
the tents throughout nearly the whole of the night, every
volley being answered by a return one from our pickets,
which no doubt knocked a few of them over; fortunately
for us no one was hurt on our side. Next morning, information was brought in by our spies, that large numbers of the
Kumber Kheyls, Ali Kheyls, Shinwarri's and other tribes,
had combined together for the purpose of helping the Zukka
Kheyls, to drive the hated kafirs out of their country. The
whole combination numbered several thousand men, and
as they had already taken up a very strong position, behind
rocks, sungas, &c., on the heights at the extreme end of the
valley, a column made up from all the regiments in
camp, together with the four mountain guns, was at once
ordered to go out and give them battle, which on arriving
within about a mile of the enemy's position, was met by
several volleys from a party who were concealed behind
a low hill, a few hundred yards away; this salute was
at once answered by a volley from our men, which quickly
scattered the enemy and made them run and take shelter,
with their main body behind the sungas. As soon as the
column got within reach of the enemies jezails, a very
heavy fire was opened upon it from the heights, and the
battle now began in earnest. A portion of the force was

ordered to drive the tribes from their sungas, and while they were climbing the heights, the mountain guns were firing over their heads into the enemies' position, killing many of them. The fighting was kept up for several hours, during which time the enemy fought well, contesting every rock and sunga ; but by half past four p. m. they were completely beaten, having been driven from their position and scattered all over the hills : the column then returned to camp. Had it not been for the strength of the enemies' position, and the cover the rocks and sungas afforded them, their losses would have been very great ; but as it was, they lost over one hundred killed besides a large number of wounded. The loss on our side was 2 killed and 7 wounded. At dusk the usual pickets were posted, and the night passed quietly ; very few shots being fired, During the following morning a party was sent out to blow up some towers at the end of the valley, and on arriving there, they at once commenced buisness, but had not proceeded far with the work before they were fired upon by a number of the enemy who had been concealed a short distance away ; this was, of course, instantly answered by our men, and as in a short time the firing became very heavy, reinforcements were sent out from camp to assist them. After a while the enemy were driven off, leaving behind them several of their number who had been knocked over. The towers having all been blown up, the whole of the party then returned to camp. Our loss during this affair was one killed and 5 wounded. The night passed very quietly, and not a shot was fired into the camp although very heavy firing was going on for several hours at the end of the valley, which could not be accounted for in any other way than that the tribes had fallen out among themselves. Early next morning some of our Afghan spies were sent out to convey a message to the chiefs, which (so rumour said) was to the following effect, that if during the next two days they didn't come into camp and ask for terms, we would scour the hills for miles around, and destroy every man and village we came across. This threat seemed to have the desired effect, for when the spies came back at 4 p. m. they brought a message to the Political Officer, saying that the Chiefs had promised to come in either next day or the day after. The night passed very quietly, only one or two shots having been fired. Next morning a small column was sent out in the direction of Chora, to meet a convoy of provisions, which had been sent out from Ali Musjid for the use of the force. On their way they were fired into several times by enemies on the heights, who always received a well aimed volley in return. Having met the convoy, our men were scattered along the whole length of it ; so that, in case of it being attacked, some of them would always be near to drive off the enemy. They had not gone far on their journey back to camp, before heavy fire commenced about 500 yards in rear of the convoy. But before I go any further I might as well state that during the last few days, letters had been regularly despatched between Ali Musjid and the Bazar Valley; they were carried by a mounted Afghan, escorted by 2 or 3 Native Lancers. This mail carrying was a hard duty, for not only was the road a very difficult one, but it was also a very dangerous one, especially for such a small number of men who had daily, for many miles, to run the gauntlet of the enemy's fire ; and it was at these men (who were returning with the mail from Ali Musjid), that the firing just mentioned was directed against; as soon as it was heard, Lieutenat Hart, Royal Engineers, who happened to be in rear of the convoy, at once turned to the right about, and ran towards the men with the mail, to give them what assistance he could, and arrived just in time to prevent 2 or 3 cowardly ruffians from mutilating a wounded Lancer whose horse had been shot dead beneath him ; he was immediately followed by 12 or 14 of the 5th Fusiliers, under Sergeant Shaw, who at once opened fire on the enemy, who took to their heels and run leaving several of their number who had got hit, lying on the ground. When the last of the enemy was out of sight, Lieutenant Hart, with the help of the few of the 5th, brought the wounded sowar into camp, where the poor fellow died soon afterwards. For attacking the men who were about to mutilate the wounded Sowar, Lieutenant Hart was recommended for the Victoria Cross, which was granted to him soon afterwards. During the afternoon the Chiefs had a great confab among themselves, near a tower about 2 miles from camp ; but they not think proper to come in and make terms. The night passed very quietly. Next day, February 1st, the Chiefs still continued their confab until about 3 p. m., when they sent word that they were coming to make peace with us. Captain Tucker, the Political Officer, at once went out to meet them, and soon afterwards brought them into camp, and placed them in front of the General's tent, where they stayed for about an hour, during which time they were entertained by the Pipers of the 25th regiment, who played a number of Scotch airs, which so pleased them that they offered each piper two Cabul rupees, which were accepted. About 5 o'clock the Chiefs were conducted to a small tent, near the lines of the 24th Punjab Native Infantry, where they remained for the night. At about midnight a sepoy of the 24th Punjab Native Infantry was shot whilst on picket, and died from loss of blood before daylight. Next morning a party of coolies, escorted by a few Bengal Lancers, were out about a mile from camp, cutting grass for the horses, when they were fired upon from a low hill, by a number of tribesmen. The General hearing the firing came out of his tent and at once ordered the guns of D.-A., R. H. A., to be loaded with shell, and a volley fired into the enemy. The guns were loaded accordingly, and just at the moment they were about to be fired, the Political Officer ran out of his tent, shouting "No ! no ! don't fire ! don't fire ! There is a mistake some-. where. I will go out to them." So getting some of the chiefs together, he made them accompany him to the place where the enemy was, and on arriving there the tribesmen said they had heard that their headman had been killed by the Feringees during the night, and that they were firing on the grass cuts to avenge their deaths ; but as some of their chiefs were

now before them, of course they could see that what they had
heard was untrue. Captain Tucker, after talking to them
for awhile, returned to camp, where shortly afterwards a
conference was held (to discuss the terms of peace) which
was attended by Lieutenant General Maude, Brigadiers
Blythe, Tytler, Macpherson, the Political Officer, and the
whole of the Chiefs. After a long discussion the Chiefs
agreed to our terms, but before the conference broke up
they were told by General Maude that if one single shot was
fired during our march back, we would most assuredly
return and punish them. All the Chiefs guaranteed that not
a shot should be fired ; one of them going so far as to say
he would accompany the force to Ali Musjid, and if a shot
was fired on the away he would forfeit his head. Everything having now been settled, of course there was nothing
left to do but for the troops to return back to their respective
camps, and the majority of the men were glad of it, for during the last 7 or 8 days they had had no bread, and only half
allowance of meat. In the place of the bread they had half
baked Indian meal chippaties, which were by an Officer
nicknamed " clammy indigestables." Not a shot was fired
during the night, so early next morning the whole of the
Troops started on their return journey ; the Dhakka and
Jellalabad party leaving first, followed about half an hour
afterwards by the men from Ali Musjid and Jumrood, who
followed the usual route along the river bed. On arriving
at the village of Chora, they bivouaced (without tents) for the
night upon some high ground on the left of the stream. Next
morning, February 4th, the column continued its march, and
on arriving near Ali Musjid, the men of the 51st Regiment
Mhairwarri Battalion, 45th Native Infantry, and 2nd Goorkhas,
proceeded to their own camps ; the 5th Fusiliers and the
remainder of the force, after halting for an hour, marching
to Jumrood, where they arrived about 4 p. m. pretty well
fagged out.

In Brigade Orders next day, Lieutenant General Maude
thanked the whole of the troops, who took part in the late

operations in Bazar Valley, for the steadiness and gallantry displayed by them throughout the expedition. Adding that he did not forget the valuable services rendered by those brave men who carried the mail.

I will conclude all I have to say about the second and last expedition against the Zukka Kheyls with a few verses, which are as follows:—

Come friends now and listen, while to you I tell,
Of how we fought bravely, and beat them as well,
Some cowardly tribes of Afredees who dwell,
    In the hills to the left of the Khyber.

These tribesmen had often us much mischief wrought,
Although unto them we had never done nought.
And this is the reason that these men we fought,
    In the hills to the left of the Khyber.

To try for to rouse us bold Britisher's ire,
Into our camps, day and night, they'd often fire,
And when we'd fire back, they would quickly retire,
    To the hills at the left of the Khyber.

And often our followers they would waylay,
And often these poor unarmed men they would slay.
And then like the cowards they were run away,
    To the hills at the left of the Khyber.

They many a time did our convoys attack,
And many a valuable load they did sack.
Not contented they often camel drivers would hack,
    As they passed on their way through the Khyber.

They often did many another foul deed,
For plunder and murder was always their creed,
So to punish these ruffians it now was decreed,
    In the hills to the left of the Khyber.

At these tribes it was ordered a blow should be dealt,
So us bold British Soldiers were sent where they dwelt.
And when we got there we our presence made felt,
    In the hills to the left of the Khyber.

We had not been in the Bazar Valley long,
Before news was brought, that to tom tom and gong
The tribesmen had gathered, nigh ten thousand strong,
    In the hills to the left of the Khyber.

To raise this large number the tribes had combined,
At the end of the valley the hill sides they lined.
And the rocks and the sungas they all were behind,
  In the hills to the left of the Khyber.

As soon as this news, it was brought into camp,
We fell in at once, and were soon on the tramp.
Determined these cowardly hillmen to flamp,
  In the hills to the left of the Khyber.

Their position was strong there was not the least doubt,
And had they fought well, they for days could held out.
Though few men could be seen, there were thousands about,
  In the hills to the left of the Khyber.

And as we drew nearer, they soon let us know,
That their numbers were large, by the volleys let go.
But their firing was either too high or too low,
  In the hills to the left of the Khyber.

Now we loaded our rifles, and at them did pot,
And but for the rocks, would have killed nigh the lot.
But still as it was, we gave it to them hot,
  In the hills to the left of the Khyber.

And as not a man of us did courage lack,
We rushed to the hills, and were up in a crack.
Then us bold Sons of Mars, did these tribesmen attack,
  In the hills to the left of the Khyber.

For hours that day we like lions did fight,
And drove back our foemen from height on to height.
Till at last, like true cowards they all took to flight,
  In the hills at the left of the Khyber.

Though the tribes, they out numbered us five men to one,
We each as a Soldier, our duty well done.
Till the battle was over, and victory won,
  In the hills to the left of the Khyber.

That we lost some brave men, I am sorry to say,
Who fought like true heroes, and fell in the fray.
But the enemy lost many scores that day,
  In the hills to the left of the Khyber.

Their losses, they would have been far larger still,
But for sungas and rocks, on the side of each hill.
Behind which they croached with the greatest of skill,
  In the hills to the left of the Khyber.

These tribesmen they had been so terribly hit,
That their chiefs, they soon came into camp to submit
To whatever terms that our General thought fit,
    In the hills to the left of the Khyber.

The terms being settled, we left the next morn,
And were well on our journey when daylight did dawn,
Though the road back was rough, we obstructions did scorn,
    In the hills to the left of the Khyber.

And now ere I close. For the bold Fusiliers,
And the rest of our Soldiers, give three hearty cheers.
May the tribesmen remember the British for years,
    In the hills to the left to the Khyber.

May each man who came back to camp safe and well,
When his friends and relations this story does tell.
Ne'er forget those brave men, who for Old England fell,
    In the hills to the left of the Khyber.

During the next week or two things went on much the same as they did before the expedition, the same old routine of guards, pickets, convoys, road-making, and mending, still went on from day to day. The weather had now changed from cold to wet, which was the cause of a great deal of fever and dysentry among the Troops, and also caused great mortality among the baggage aminals, which were dying in even larger numbers than they did during the cold and frost.

On the 13th of February Wali Mahomed passed through Jumrood on his way to Jellalabad : this man was the Afghan General who commanded the Ameer's troops at the battle of Piewar Kotal in the Kurrum Valley. Here when he saw his men were getting beaten, he left them in the lurch and gave himself up to the British ; at the same time swearing that if they would accept his services, he would do all he could to bring about an understanding between the Ameer and the Indian Government; but as a few days afterwards the Ameer fled to Turkistan (where he died shortly afterwards), of course his services were not then required, so he was kept in India until the time I write when he was on his way to join General Sir Sam. Brown, as it was thought he might be useful in influencing the new Ameer (Yacoob Khan) to come to terms.

On February 24th, Sir Frederick Haines, the Commander-in-Chief, passed through Jumrood. He was on a tour of inspection, and was accompanied by several military men of high rank, and all his Staff. All along the road, between the fort and Makeson's road, in the Pass, were posted small parties of the 5th Fusiliers, about 200 yards apart, for the purpose of preventing anything from happening to His Excellency as he passed by; between these parties of the 5th were also posted, about 20 yards apart, men of the newly raised Afredee levy—the Jezailchi Corps, or Tucker's Brigade, as they are sometimes called, from the fact that they were raised by Captam Tucker from the tribes round about the hills near Jumrood, for the purpose of keeping open the pass during the passage of convoys, &c. They are armed with old muskets and Enfield rifles, and as long as there are other troops to watch them they do what is required off them; but during the night they do a bit of marauding on their own account. It was the duty of each individual man, as the Commander-in-Chief passed by, to present arms to him, which they did but in a way that plainly said they would much rather cut his throat. On the return of the Commander-in-Chief on March 7th, the 5th Fusiliers furnished a Guard of Honour to recieve him; it was composed of nearly one hundred picked men, and I am sure a finer looking body of soldiers never went to guard the Queen.

For some time past a large gang of marauders have been giving a deal of trouble, by firing into the camp at night, murdering camp-followers who have strayed a short distance away, stealing camels and cutting up their drivers, and committing many other depredations. It is customary in Jumrood to send all the camels (not required for the daily convoy) to graze at the foot of the hills round about; they are generally taken out 3 or 4 miles, and sometimes there are so many of them that they form a string nearly a mile in length, and as they are only escorted by a few Bengal Lancers (who cannot be at every part of the line at once) these marauders watch their opportunity, and when they see a part of the line unprotected, they swoop down upon it, cut up the camel walas and drive as many camels as they can into the hills; and if the Sowars should follow them very likely another gang will come down while they are away, and carry off a lot more. On one occasion they cut a camel wala's head off, wounded another, and got away with eight camels; on another occasion they killed four camel walas, wounded several others, and carried off over 30 camels. Besides these two instances they have committed many others lately. But these robbers don't always have it their own way, for sometimes the Lancers are to quick for them, and then if they don't get knocked over they are made prisoners and brought into camp. A great many of them have been brought in lately and tried, but they are generally dealt too lightly with; the majority of them are either let off with a flogging, or a term of imprisonment. As this system of punishment was found to work very badly, it was determined if any more prisoners were brought in they should be shot. The first batch brought in after this determination had been come to, was a party of five. It seems the camels were out grazing as usual on March 11th, escorted by the Lancers, when all at once about 30 of these ruffians swooped down upon them, and after wounding several of the camel walas, attempted to carry off a number of camels; but they reckoned without their host this day, for the Sowars came down on them before they could get into the hills, and after several of them had been knocked over, the remainder (with the exception of the five just mentioned, who were made prisoners) took to their heels and ran for their lives. As soon as the five prisoners were brought into camp they were taken before the Provost Martial and tried there and then, and having been found guilty of the charge, four of them were sentenced to be shot, and the remaining one to receive 50 lashes with the cat. One of the men that was to be shot was suffering from a lance wound in the back, which bled to such an extent that

he died from loss of blood during the night, and so saved
the Government a few rounds of ammunition. Early next
morning, at the bottom of a low hill, a few hundred yards
from camp, three graves were dug, and alongside of these
stood three upright posts, about 7 feet high. At 7 o'clock,
the condemned men, escorted by a number of the 24th
Punjab Native Infantry, were brought to the place of execution
and at once pinioned to the posts. One of them was only a
young fellow about 17, but no doubt was as hardened to
crime as the other two, who were both ruffianly looking cut-
throats. All three of them took it very cool and one of them
refused to be blindfolded, but he was blindfolded all the
same. All being in readiness, the firing party, which consisted of a party of the 5th Fusiliers, at once came to the
front and took up a position about 10 paces away from the
condemned men, and the order was then given, "Fire a volley
with ball cartridge, ready." Just at this moment the man
who had refused to be blindfolded, by some means or other
slipped the bandage from his eyes down on to his throat,
and as he did so he raised his eyes upwards and shouted in
a loud clear voice in Pushto, "my god, my god, I am innocent."
He had hardly said the last word before the word "Present"
was given, and bang went the volley, the next instant their
riddled bodies were cut down from the posts and thrown
into the graves, and there they were buried almost before
the breath of life had fled. Soon after the execution the
other ruffian received his 50 lashes and was then turned out
of camp, and told to go to his tribe and tell them how he and
his companions had been dealt with by the Kafirs. On the
same day when the Bengal Lancers went out to escort the
camels to graze, they were accompanied by a company of
the 5th Fusiliers, who were going out to attack a village,
whose inhabitants were supposed to have had a hand in the
late outrages. On our men nearing the village, the people
suspecting they had come to punish them, at once set fire
to everything that would burn, and fled to the hills, which
saved the trouble of clearing them out. Next day, March

13th, Lieutenant General Maude issued an order, which was to the following effect :—That all tribesmen caught in the act of robbing or murdering our followers, attacking convoys, stealing camels, or even attempting to commit any of these or similar outrages, were not to be made prisoners but shot on the spot. This order seemed to have the desired effect, for things went along very quietly during the remaining few days we were in Jumrood. On March 16th the 5th Fusiliers were ordered to leave Jumrood and march for Basawal next morning ; but as it rained all night and during the three following days, it was not till the morning of the 20th that anything could be done. On this day there was a complete change in the weather, where everything during the last few weeks had been wet, gloom, and fog, all was now sunshine ; and with the sun came the beginning of the hot season. The tents having been struck and loaded, the regiment commenced its journey, marching along the usual route up the pass. During the last few weeks the rocks had been blasted near Ali Musjid, and a good road made right into the camp, so that there was no need now to wade through the stream. On arriving at the camp, the tents were pitched and the men soon settled down. Since we came back from the last Bazar Valley expedition, an interesting discovery has been made near the camp, in the shape of three beautiful tombs. They were discovered in rather a curious manner. Some men were one day strolling across the top of a small hill when one of them saw what he thought was the top of a skull sticking up through the ground, so he set to work and uneathered it, when it turned out to be a splendidly shaped head made of hard cement. The man thinking this was rather a curious thing to find in such an outlandish place, took his prize down into camp, where it was seen by an Engineer Officer, who, fancying there might be other things beneath the top of the hill, applied for permission to commence excavating, which was granted ; and gaving mustered the sappers and miners, the work was begun at once. In the course of a few days, parts of statues, ancient walls, and the three tombs were brought to light; and besides these, many old coins were found, which proved the remains to be at least 1700 years' old. The statues were all in pieces, but the walls and tombs were in a state of first class preservation, and looked as if they had only lately been erected. The walls are built of common pieces of rock strongly cemented together. The tombs are each about 4 feet high, 6 feet broad, and 10 or 12 feet long, and all of them are beautifully decorated with small models of the idol Budda, which are very nicely coloured, and look as bright as if they had been painted but yesterday. To many a learned man at home these Buddist remains would be full of interest. They are guarded night and day by Native Soldiers, and very few Europeans pass through Ali Musjid without going to see them. Besides these relics and the Fort, there is very little else of interest to be seen ; and take Ali Musjid altogether it is a place where very few people care for stopping more than a day or two, surrounded as it is by lofty hills, from whose tops ruffianly Afreedes are continually firing into the camp ; troubled with plagues of fleas, flies, and mosquitoes, and reeking with the bodies of dead camels, whose rotting carcasses smell anything but sweet. It is a very undersirable place to stay in for any length of time. I have a few verses by me, which I copied from one of the Indian daily papers, and which I think must have been written by some one who is at present stationed here. They are as follows :—

Let us hope, o'er the Khyber's rough passes,
Sweet peace will soon look down and smile,
And a sound it may stop, which alas ! is
The boom of the nasty jezail.
Oh ! soon may the campaign be over,
At present our hearts they do bleed
While we're camping, but scarcely in clover,
    At Ali Musjid.

Rough crags and tall summits frown o'er us,
The stream murmers softly below,
But its song from the rocks soft and porous,
Bears onward a burden of woe.
·Oh! thus far escaped from the slaughter.
Our fate is most cruel indeed.
We must drink antimonial water,
     At Ali Musjid.

Alas! that hard fate should allot us
So much of humanity's ills;
Our enemies steadily pot us
By day and by night from the hills.
While the smell that assails our poor noses—
Long suffering organs indeed—
Differs strongly from atter of roses,
     At Ali Musjid.

Round our camp in thick groups, alternating
With refuse of camel and byle,
Lie the dead and the fetid, creating
A depot of ev'rything vile.
Fierce rays from the sun overpower us,
Disease sows its quick springing seed,
Flies by day, fleas by night, nigh devour us,
     At Ali Musjid.

Then our tots undergo diminution
Most strangely ere coming to hand,
And the rum's in a state of dilution,
No right-minded Briton could stand.
While we dine in the poorest camp fashion,
Oh! scanty and coarse is the feed.
For we're strictly confined to our ration,
     At Ali Musjid.

Oh! soon may the day of glad tidings
Dawn bright o'er our suffering band,
When we'll hush our complainings and chidings,
And march from this desolate land.
When we'll burst through our present vile trammels,
And revel exultant and freed
From the horrible odour of camels,
    At Ali Musjid.

Leaving Ali Musjid next morning, the Regiment continued its journey up the pass, which for the first two miles is
very narrow; its sides being composed of tremendous high
rocks with large pieces jutting out of them, which seemed as if
they were going to fall and crush those beneath them. The
road during this distance was very bad, the men having to
wade through the stream several times, and march over stones
of all sizes. The pass now gets wider, and ascends until it
reaches Lundi Kotal, which is 3,500 feet above the sea. At
this place a splendid view was obtained of the large range
of mountains called the Hindoo Khoosh, which, with their
snowy peaks, reared high above the clouds, and dazzling in
the sun's rays, looked beautiful indeed. In the wider parts
of the pass are several villages and a few small patches of
cultivated ground. Passing Lundi Kotal the road is cut in
the sides of a number of large and rocky hills, and for three
miles it descends until it reaches Lundi Khana, running in a
very zigzag manner all the way; the scenery along it is
extremely rugged, there being nothing but large hills and high
and jagged rocks on the one side and deep chasms and
ravines on the other. This road is extremely dangerous on
account of its narrowness and the number of sudden turn-
ings, and several accidents have already occurred. This
day's march has been a very hot and tiresome one, and it was
nearly 7 p. m. before the baggage guard (who were in rear
of everything) arrived at Lundi Khana. The cause of this
delay was the half starved and worn out nature of the baggage animals; over thirty of them dropping down on the

road from sheer exhaustion—unable to go an inch further.
A dying camel is a most pathetic sight : the poor beast dies
in harness, carrying his load to the death, and then when he
cannot bear the burden no longer, he sits or rather drops
down with his legs under him, and never moves again until
the moment that death comes to his relief, when he falls
over to one side, gives a low moan and a few convulsive
struggles and is no more. Leaving Lundi Khana next
morning we commenced our march towards Dhakka. For
the first five miles the country is extremely wild and barren,
and a more desolate looking region I have never before seen.
Here the pass comes to an end and we now enter what is
called Dhakka plain : at the further end, about 4 miles away,
stands Dhakka Fort, near which, on arriving, the regiment
pitched their tents. This Fort is a very large one, being over
a mile in circumference ; it is square in shape with a large
bastion at each corner, it has a good sized bungalow in the
centre, and is divided into several parts by large mud walls. It
stands on the right bank of the Cabul river. On the opposite
bank is the city of Lalpoora, which is ruled by a Khan who
has done us some service both against the Ameer's troops
on their retreat from Ali Musjid and in providing guides to
our Forces in their expeditions to Bazar Valley. Soon after
the tents were pitched, firing was heard about a mile across
the plain in the direction of the pass, and as the whole of the
regimental baggage had not yet arrived, it was feared that a
gang of loosewalas had come down upon it, with the intention of carrying it off. A party of Native Lancers were sent
out to ascertain the cause of the firing, and on arriving near
the spot where it proceeded from, they came upon a large
number of robbers, just commencing to loot the baggage,
which unfortunately seems to have been very ill-guarded.
The Sowars at once opened fire and the robbers made off
(without taking anything with them) closely followed by
the Lancers, who, after a smart chase, knocked several of
them over and made 21 prisoners. These prisoners they
brought into Dhakka Fort, and handed them over to a strong

guard, who placed them in a large tent and surrounded them with sentries. What punishment was meted out to these ruffians I cannot tell; but I suppose they shared the same fate as a good many more of the same class, *i. e.* being sent about their business, with a rupee and a blanket a few days afterwards, no doubt to trouble us again some other time. Towards evening 100 men of the 5th Fusiliers went into the fort on detachment. Early next morning the regiment started for Basawal. For several miles the country around was rocky, wild, and extremely barren. After going about half way, some villages were passed and around these was a large amount of cultivated land, covered with crops of growing corn. A short distance further on, the country again became barren, and for the last 4 miles the road on each side was lined with thousands of graves. I never saw so many in all my life. If there was one I should think there were 30,000. This truly was a city of the dead. The marching this day was very wearisome, as the road for the best part of the way was covered with stones, which made it very uncomfortable under foot; the men also felt the heat very much. On arriving at Basawal, the tents of the regiment were pitched near those of the troops already there; a few hours afterwards it was ordered that an expedition was to start in the evening, to punish a section of the powerful Shinwarri tribe, who lived in a number of large villages called Dea Surak on the lower slopes of the Safed Koh, about 13 or 14 miles to the left of the camp, for outrages they had committed on small parties of our people on several different occasions. On the first occasion they attacked a small party of the 17th regiment who had gone out from Basawal, escorting a large number of camels, which were sent out to graze near the above villages. The camels had not been grazing long, before fifty or sixty of the Shinwarris came out of the villages and treacherously fired a volley into the escort, killing two men and wounding another. On the second occasion they attacked a surveying party and wounded an officer, and on the last occasion they fired on a commisariat agent who had gone to Dea Surak to purchase forage. In fact they seemed determined that none of our people should come near them at all. So just to let them see that they could not trifle with the British for nothing, and to thrash them for the outrages they had committed, it was decided to send this expedition against them. The troops composing the expeditionary force, consisted of 150 men of the 5th Fusiliers, under Major Taylor; 250 men of the 17th Regiment, under Colonel Utterson; one squadron of the 13th Bengal Lancers, under Captain Thompson; one troop 11th Bengal Lancers, under Lieutenant Heath; one company of 2nd Ghoorkhas, under Captain Becher; one company of 27th Native Infantry, under Lieutenant Thruston; and two guns of 11-9th R. A. The whole under the command of Brigadier General Tytler, with Major Gordon as Brigade Major, and Major Conolly as Political Officer. This force was drawn up about 10 P. M., and shortly afterwards moved off in dead silence. The night being very dark, and the road much broken by water-courses and rough ground, the pace was slow, and considerable delay was caused by frequent breaks in the column. However, after a hard march, the troops arrived at some low hills near the villages and halted. At day-light the Shinwarris made their appearance in great force and at once commenced firing. Two companies of the 5th and two of the 17th were ordered to advance, and soon drove the enemy back across a nullah on the right of our position. The cavalry meanwhile crept quietly round a bend in the nullah, and remained there for a time awaiting a favourable opportunity to charge. Looking from the opposite side of the nullah a movement was now seen amongst the enemy, and it was very evident that they intended to make another rush towards the Infantry, which they did a moment or two afterwards; but were again driven back by the fire from the Martinis, which had a great effect upon them for a while. After a time a large number plucked up courage and again came forward to within 50 yards of the nullah where the cavalry were, whom it was very evident they now saw, for deliberately kneeling they fired a volley right among the Sowars, with better intention than direction, as but one Sowar was killed and some minor injuries inflicted. The next moment they turned to the right about and attempted to retire; but their chance was lost, for a few seconds later the cavalry broke into a gallop and rushed with irresistable force right into the midst of them, driving all before them with lance and sabre. The Sowars, after riding right through the enemy, wheeled about and charged back again, and many hand to hand encounters took place. No one looking on could question the pluck of these Shinwarris, who now stood their ground until literally ridden over, each man either firing his jezail or doing his best with his tulwar. When many of them had been placed *hors de combat* the remainder fled to the high ground near the hills, and the Infantry coming up at this moment opened fire and completed the rout. The mule Battery now came into play and made good practice at small parties assembled on the adjacent hills; on more than one occasion, a shell was seen to burst in the midst of a group, who, no doubt, imagined themselves secure at a distance of a thousand yards. A small party of cavalry went out to the right front about 10 a. m. for the purpose of meeting a jirgah, but after waiting for some time, Major Conolly, the Political Officer, returned without achieving his object. Preparations were now made to blow up the towers and burn the villages, and during the time this work was going on hardly a shot was fired. About 1 P. M. the order was given to retire towards Pesh Bolak. Our men had not got far on their return journey before about 3,000 of the enemy came down from the hills and followed the force over the broken ground, firing their jezails and yelling frightfully; one party of fanatics, sword in hand even attempting to charge a Company of the 5th Fusiliers—a move that was very promptly checked. As the column had now reached pretty open ground near Pesh Bolak, the Shinwarris did not follow any further, but stopped all at once and fired a *fue de joie* as a parting salute. General Tytler now gave orders for all the troops to continue their march to Basawal, with the exception of the 27th Native

Infantry and the 2nd Ghoorkhas, who remained under his command in Pesh Bolak for the night, the inhabitants fearing that after the column had passed the Shinwarris might attack them for being friendly towards us. Nothing more of note took place, and the force reached Basawal about 5 P. M., pretty well knocked up after all the hard work they had done. It had been expected in Basawal that the troops would have returned to camp before midday, and in anticipation of this the tents and baggage belonging to the men of the 17th regiment were sent early in the morning to Bari Kab, where the Detachment was expected to arrive during the afternoon. But as has been seen the troops did not get back till 5 o'clock, when it was too late and the men were too tired to proceed any further. So it was decided to allow the 17th to remain in Basawal for the night. Spare tents were pitched for them by the 5th Fusiliers, who did what they could for them, bringing them tea, lending them blankets, and trying to make them as comfortable as possible. For these little attentions the 17th seemed very thankful, and many of them said they would never forget the kindness they had received from the 5th Fusiliers. General Tytler and his small force, who had remained in Pesh Bolak, passed the night unmolested and returned to Basawal next morning. This expedition is considered to have been most ably conducted, and the whole of the operations most successfully carried out. It is calculated that the Shinwarris lost in killed and wounded at least 400 men, and this is considered by many to be too low an estimate. The losses on our side are extremely small, being 3 men and 2 horses killed, and 6 men and 5 horses wounded. As I have a few verses about this affair I will now bring them forward—

THE BATTLE OF DEA SURAK.

Who says that Britain's sons are not the same men as of old,
  Who says that when a foe they meet, that they act far from bold.
And who is it says they're afraid for Old England to bleed,
  And that they are not like the men who fought at Runnymede.
To those who say such things as these, I ask let them look back,
  To the great and glorious battle lately fought at Dea Surak.

To forage among the villages some of our men they went,
  But fiercely the Shinwarris rose, and volleys at them sent.
And as they were outnumbered, back to camp they wound their way.
  While deadly vows of swift revenge were registered that day.
And soon a force full well equipped, these tribesmen to attack,
  At midnight gathered near the hills that rise by Dea Surak.

'Twas silence all till morning's light dawned bright above the snow,
  Then fiercely sprang to arms our men, and fiercely rose the foe.
Led forward by their Moolahs, shouting forth the prophet's word,
  These tribesmen rushed towards our men, with jezail, shield and sword.
But soon they felt the bullet's sting, which quickly drove them back,
  And many of them bit the dust that day at Dea Surak.

But still these foemen were not beat, for soon they turned again
  Against our gallant Infantry, and fought with might and main.
But they were no match for our men, whose aim was true and low,
  And soon full length upon the plain lay many a reckless foe.
They stood their ground courageously, their pluck none can deny,
  And midst the din of battle raised to Allah many a cry.
While rising o'er fanatic shouts, the rifle's deadly crack,
  Soon hushed the quaint jezails full note, that day at Dea Surak.

But hark the sound of ringing hoops, who sweep across the plains,
  With turbans floating in the wind, bare swords and tightened reins.
Their fiery chargers streaked with foam, as wildly on they dash.
  Their sabres poised to deal a blow, swift as the lightning's flash.
These are the native cavalry, advancing to attack,
  And soon with dead and wounded strew the ground at Dea Surak.

The tribesmen once more turn about, and to the hills they run,
  Which bring the battle to an end, a hard fought day is won.
And glad are we, that on our side there were but few to die,
  Though several hundreds of our foes upon the plain do lie.
Our soldiers now fall in and then commence their journey back.
  And soon some miles have left behind the field of Dea Surak.

The officers and rank and file deserve their country's praise,
  For well they for Old England fought, her martial fame to raise.
Then let us hope that every man, who came back from the fray,
  May for his Queen and country live to fight for many a day.
To those who run our Soldiers down, I ask let them look back
  To the great and glorious battle that was fought at Dea Surak.

After the return of our men from the expedition they settled down to the old routine of guards and pickets, convoy duty, escorting the baggage animals to graze, &c. One company of the 5th were sent on detachment to Bari Kab, which is a small fort about 12 miles away towards Jellalabad. For several weeks every available man not on duty, was employed digging trenches and gunpits, building breastworks and other fortifications round the camp. On April 6th, one of our men named Moran, was stabbed in the side by an Afghan fanatic in the Pushto Bazar. He was getting his boots nailed, and was in a stooping position at the time when the fanatic came behind him and drawing a long knife from beneath his kapra, treacherously stabbed him in the right side, inflicting a wound about three inches deep, which though serious was not fatal, as the man recovered his usual health sometime afterwards. As soon as the fanatic had committed the deed he attempted to stab another man of the 5th, who happened to be standing by, but luckily he did not succeed. He was at once surrounded, disarmed and taken before the Provost Martial, who asked him why he did the crime, and he said that God told him to do it. He was kept tied to a post all night with sentries over him, and next morning was tried by Court Martial, and sentenced to be shot in the evening. He took it very cool and walked boldly to the place of execution. After he was pinioned the sentence was carried out, and shortly afterwards his body was burned and the ashes scattered to the winds, as a warning to other fantaics who were known to be prowling about. A few days later another of our men was stabbed at Bari Kab. A fanatic crept up behind him, and with a spear on the end of a stick, stabbed him in the lower part of the back, inflicting a very serious wound, which has made the man an invalid for life. After committing the crime the fanatic ran away, but was chased and shot down, and his body afterwards burnt.

I think now we had better go back to Dhakka, and see how the 100 men of the 5th have been getting along there. After settling down in the fort they were employed on the usual duties, and nothing happened that is worth mentioning until the 21st of April, when news was brought that a powerful tribe, called the Momunds, were in arms. The parti-

culars of this rising are as follows : For a long time an uneasy
feeling has prevailed among a large tribe called the Momunds (who had hitherto been on good terms with us), due
partly to their personal affections for Yacoob Khan, which
they never exhibited for the late Shere Ali ; and partly, it is
said, to the exhortations of one Fakir Sahib, who is endea-
vouring to raise a religious war against the Feringi. Reports
of a various and conflicting nature had reached the British
authorities at Fort Dhakka ; and assumed a more definite
shape when a party of headmen from a large village called
Kam Dhakka, came into the Fort on April 21st with the
information that a large body of Momunds were beginning
to cross the Cabul river, with the intention of first destroying
their village, for being friendly towards the British, and when
that was completed of openly attacking Dhakka Fort. The
headmen implored the authorities to send troops at once
to help them to repel the Momund attack. This request was
at once granted, and they were told to go back and defend
their village until our troops arrived there, which would be
as soon as possible. Accordingly they went back, and
shortly afterwards Captain O. Moore Creagh, with two companies of the Mhairwari Battalion, started in the direction of
Kam Dhakka, with orders to render any necessary assistance
to the well disposed villages on this the south, or right bank of
the river. To his great astonishment on arrival the straight-
ened villagers declined to have any thing to say to his
force ; and to make things worse they (with the assistance of
the Momunds that had already crossed) actually attacked him,
and tried to drive him back across the plain, but were un-
successful. As it was now getting dark, there was nothing
for it but to retire to the nearest hill, throw up breastworks, post
his little force behind them, and await events and the dawn
of the ensuing day, and then determine on further proceedings.
He was attacked several times during the night ; but on all
occasions was able to drive the enemy back. The dawn of
the 22nd showed his position to be surrounded by about
1,500 Momunds, who, during the morning made several

most determined attacks upon him and his little force, but by Captain Creagh's gallantry, and his men making good use of their ammunition and at times charging with the bayonet, these attacks were always successfully repelled. As the enemy seemed to gather fresh strength as the day wore on, and as owing to the nature of the ground it would have been exceedingly difficult to have retired without being greatly harrassed by his opponents, it was determined to send to Fort Dhakka for reinforcements. One of the few sowars accompanying the force was accordingly despatched for assistance : and gallantly he performed his task, the chances of his reaching the Fort without coming to grief being very remote, but at any rate he succeeded, and reinforcements were promptly despatched under Major Barnes, 10th Bengal Lancers, consisting of a Detachment of his own regiment, about 80 men of the 5th Fusiliers, under Captain Ormond, and a portion of the Mhairwarri Corps. This instalment had to fight their way through the Momunds, and reached Captain Creagh soon after midday. Arriving not a moment too soon either, for the Mhairwarris had hardly a round of ammunition left, and were showing signs of exhaustion, and it could be plainly seen that they could not have held out much longer against the host of Momunds in front of them, who now numbered over 2,000. Major Barnes' force soon altered the state of affairs, as all were now enabled to resume the offensive, which they did with great determination, scattering the Momunds in all directions, the majority of them taking to the hills, where a great deal of skirmishing went on for several hours between them and our men who had followed them up. Towards evening a further reinforcement arrived from Lundi Kotal : this consisted of 200 men of Her Majesty's 12th Regiment, and 2 mountain guns. The guns at once came into action and together with the Infantry fire soon cleared the hills, and at dusk very few of the enemy were to be seen, although no doubt hundreds of them were lurking about in caves and behind rocks. As darkness was now setting in and as it was thought that nothing would be gained by the troops bivouacing for the night where it was, it was decided by the Senior Officer present to march at once to Fort Dhakka. The march back had hardly commenced before the Momunds, as is their wont, began to follow, and commenced firing at the men in rear, and in the darkness caused some confusion, but beyond that doing little or no damage. Dhakka was reached about 9 p. m., and this concluded the business, with the exception of a reconnaissance made the following day, when no sign of the enemy was discovered, save a raft load of them being towed across the river, the other side of which they never reached, for a well directed shell from a field gun promptly sent the whole lot of them to the bottom. Our casualties were : 5th Fusiliers, 2 Sergeants wounded ; 12th Regiment, 2 men killed and 3 wounded ; Mhairwarri Battalion, 3 Havildars killed and 13 rank and file wounded. It is impossible to say what the loss was on the Momund side, owing to the rough an hilly nature of the ground over which most of the fighting took place ; but the lowest computation it could not have been less than 100 killed and wounded. Captain Creagh, for the gallant way in which he led his Mhairwarris, was recommended for the Victoria Cross; and I am happy to say it was shortly afterwards granted to him. Here are a few verses about this brush with the Momunds :

Who came and asked for British aid,
To help them stop the Momund raid,
Which was that evening to be made,
 The people of Kam Dhakka.

Who gladly their assistance gave,
And sent forth men both true and brave,
These people and their homes to save,
 The British at Fort Dhakka.

Who when the staunch Mhairwarris came,
Turned treacherously against the same,
And tried to drive them 'cross the plain,
 The people at Kam Dhakka.

Who when these men the Momunds joined,
Threw up breastworks and got behind,
And quickly then these breastworks lined,
    The Mhairwarris at Kam Dhakka.

Who when the Momunds did attack,
Like brave men quickly hurled them back,
And who did not true courage lack,
    The Mhairwarris at Kam Dhakka.

Who fought like tigers when at bay,
From evening until noon next day,
When led by gallant Captain Creagh,
    The Mhairwarris at Kam Dhakka.

Who made two thousand tribesmen reel,
And also made these hordes to feel,
The powerful force of British steel,
    The Mhairwarris at Kam Dhakka.

Who came with other troops that day,
And thought the Momunds fought their way,
To help these gallant men at bay,
    The Fifth did at Kam Dhakka.

Who got there just in time to save,
This band of staunch Mhairwarris brave,
From meeting an untimely grave,
    The Fifth did at Kam Dhakka.

Who did not for the British care,
Until the British they came there,
When quickly they were made to stare,
    The Momunds at Kam Dhakka.

Who then attacked the Momund clan,
That was that day led by their Khan,
And fought them fairly every man,
    Our Soldiers at Kam Dhakka.

Who did these tribesmen's courage chill,
And followed them from hill to hill,
And many of these men did kill,
    Our Soldiers at Kam Dhakka.

Who all the Momund host defied,
And quickly lowered their foemen's pride,
And some of them like heroes died,
    Our Soldiers at Kam Dhakka.

Who did like men most bravely fight,
From mid-day until dark at night,
And knew full well their cause was right,
    Our Soldiers at Kam Dhakka.

Who often mid the battle's fray,
Thought of Old English far away,
And for her won a hard fought day,
    Our Soldiers at Kam Dhakka.

And when at home this tale we tell,
We'll think of those who fought so well,
And for their country nobly fell,
    At the Battle of Kam Dhakka.

As everything is now quiet round about Dhakka we will return again to head-quarters in Basawal. The 23rd of April being Saint George's day, and Saint George being the patron Saint of the regiment, of course we could not let it pass without commemorating it in some kind of manner, so it was determined by several of our men to celebrate it by having an Ethiopean entertainment in the evening, which under our able Drum Major's management turned out a great success. Everybody that was present being convulsed with laughter at the quaint songs, witty sayings, and funny doings of the " Afghan Minstrels," as the entertainers had styled themselves. Next day garrison sports were held on a flat piece of ground just outside the camp, at which there was any amount of running, jumping, throwing the cricket

ball, pony racing, tent pegging, spearing the Afghan, and
other sports. The men of the 5th who competed, keeping
up the credit of the old corps by the excellent manner in
which they acquitted themselves, especially those who took
part in the tug of war against the 9th Lancers, which was a
tug and no mistake. Several other Garrison sports took
place during our stay in Basawal, all of which were thoroughly
enjoyed by those who were able to be present. The
weather was now getting very hot indeed, and living in the
thin pall tents was almost intolerable. Hot winds like a
blast from a furnace now began to blow, and sand and dust
storms were of hourly occurrence. Besides these we were
tormented by myriads of flies and mosquitoes, which made
us anything but sweet tempered. Disease also made its
appearance, and a great many men were soon down with fever
and dysentry. We lost two young officers from fever, both
of them were fine promising young men, and no doubt had
they but have been spared, would have made a name for
themselves. It is said that troubles never come alone, and
in our case it was quite true ; for besides the hot winds, sand
storms, flies and mosquitoes, we were visited every night
by band of greasy skinned gentlemen called loosewalas.
They were the most daring thieves that ever robbed a camp.
They would come prowling around about midnight, stark
naked and greased all over, and in spite of extra Sentries
and other precautions, they often managed to get into the
camp and carry off booty. But they were not always successful, for on several occasions their presence was discovered
and many of them were shot by the Sentries. There
was also another class of robbers who used to prowl round
about Basawal. They were called the wire pullers, from
the fact that they made a habit of taking the telegraph wire
from the poles and carrying off a mile or two of it nightly.
What these robbers did with it I dont know; but I heard
that a party of them took about twenty miles of it to Cabul
and presented it to the new Ameer, as a token of their
respect for him and their hatred of the British. On one

occasion some loosewalas stole three donkeys off a friendly native. The man had just brought a load of wood to the commissariat, and was returning to his village when he was set upon not far away from camp by three of these robbers, who, after chasing him for a short distance towards the camp, leisurely turned and walked off with one donkey each. He came into camp and reported the circumstance there and then, and three or four Sowars were at once sent in pursuit, and as it was daylight they soon came up to the blokes with the mokes, and in a few seconds each of these gentlemen was minus his head, and the donkeys were saved. The cavalrymen brought the heads into camp and showed them to several of our men, one of whom remarked that the eyes were staring very much. " Ah ! said his comrade, and no wonder. Its enough to make a man stare when he loses his head for stealing a donkey." Rumours were frequently going the round of the camp, that the tribes had combined together to attack us. Sometimes 5,000 men had gathered together in one direction, 3,000 in another, 2,000 in another, and so on. All of whom seemed to disappear as suddenly as they had gathered. Although it was often expected that they would attack the camp, they never did do so. Things went along in this manner for several weeks. In the meantime the 100 men that were in Dhakka Fort, having been relieved by a party of the 12th Regiment, had rejoined head-quarters, and the company that was in Bari Kab, having been relieved by another company of the regiment, had also rejoined. On May 13th a draft from England, of about 100, joined the regiment. These men had had a very weary march up country, and had unfortunately lost several of their number from cholera on the road. As it was thought very undesirable to send them to their companies, for fear of spreading the infection, they were ordered to encamp by themselves on the plain, about six hundred yards away. On the 18th the regiment was served out with large European privates double-topped tents, and not one moment before they were wanted, for every day the heat naturally gets fiercer, and the flies and mosquitoes if possible more exasperating. The sand and dust storms still continue to blow with unceasing fury, and it is impossible to get a morsel of clean food, dust and dirt being in everything. We eat dirt, drink dirt, and sleep in dirt, in fact dirt seems to be part of ourselves; and really believe that when we get clean again we shall feel quite uncomfortable. I have heard say that each grown up person during their lifetime eats on an average a peck of dirt. But I think that each grown up person, here in Basawal, has during the last few weeks eaten several bushels. The hot winds still continue and are hotter than ever, almost singeing the hair off one's head, and fever, dysentry and cholera are claiming fresh victims daily. Considering there are hundreds of dead camels rotting round about the camp, no one can wonder at it.

A correspondent in a letter to the *Pioneer*, speaking of Basawal, says :—The heat here is something terrible, and several Officers have already been knocked up from it. Within the last few days, four, including Colonel McIntyre, V. C., 2nd Ghoorkhas, have been invalided back to India, and several others that are sick will shortly follow. Miles of this tract of country reminds one forcibly of Dore's pictures of the Infernal Regions; in fact one is often inclined to think that the proverbial thin sheet of paper has got worn through in these parts. On May 19th, on account of so much sickness in the regiment, we were ordered in the evening to shift camp about a mile further up the plain. As soon as the tents were pitched one of our men went back to the head-quarters camp and foolishly stayed there until after dark. He then started to come back again, but was waylaid and murdered by some of the blood.thirsty ruffians that prowl about at night. His body was found quite naked, in rear of the camp early next morning: he looked a dreadful sight, and to all appearances had been shot in the back; the bullet passing through his heart and out of his left breast. His clothing must then have been taken off and the front part of his body dreadfully gashed, crosswise, from the neck downwards. Although every one in camp was sorry for his untimely end, a great many said he was the cause of his own death by being away from camp after dark. On the 20th, on account of desease being about, the whole of the sick and about half the troops left Basawal, and went to a place called Markob, about six miles away. Our Regiment, with the exception of two companies, remaining where it was. On the 26th the treaty of peace was signed in General Sir Sam. Brown's camp at Gundamuck, between the new Ameer Yacoob Khan, on the one side, and Major Cavagnari, (as the representative of the Indian Government, on the other. The terms of the treaty are follows :—

All Afghan territory, as far as Lundi Kotal in the Khyber Pass, the Piewar Kotal in the Kurrum Valley, and the country above Quetta, as far as and including Candahar, were to become part of British India. The Ameer is to allow a British Envoy to reside permantly at Cabul, and is on no account to hold any intercourse whatever with any foreign power, or their representatives, without first receiving the permission of the Indian Government. The Indian Government on their part is to pay the Ameer an annual subsidy of six lacs of rupees (£ 60,000) and are, in case of Afghanistan being invaded, to assist him with money and arms, and if necessary with troops to repel the invaders. The signing of this treaty brings the war to a close, and nothing now remains to be done but to march the troops back to India as quick as possible. No doubt, if the Government desired it, the Ameer would consent to the troops remaining in Afghanistan till the commencement of the cold season. But as every one on the Khyber line prefers running the risks of a hot march, to remaining in a country reeking with deadly diseases, it has been decided to retire at once. Accordingly on June 2nd, one Company of the 5th started on their return journey, escorting the Field Hospital, and on the same day the Draft from Markob joined head-quarters in Basawal, and were sent to their companies. On the 3rd, in Brigade Orders, Brigadier General Doran thanked us for the willing manner in which we had performed the most trying and arduous duties during the whole of the campaign. On the 4th the Regiment (excepting the Companies at Markob and Bari Kab, who followed next morning) left Basawal and marched to Dhakka, where we remained for the day. At sun set the tents were struck and packed ready for the next day's march. About midnight a Native cavalryman went mad, and commenced rushing about among the hackery-drivers and camp-followers, and frightened them so much, that a lot of them set up a hideous yell as if they were being murdered. This yell had the effect of setting other natives yelling, and in about two seconds there was nothing but screaching and howling all round the camp. To make matters worse just at this moment a dust storm burst upon us in all its fury, it came like the rush of ten thousand demons. In the darkness we naturally thought the camp was attacked and at once sprang to arms; but in a few minutes the real cause of the disturbance was found out and the mad man was secured. Everything getting quiet again, we lay down and rested till morning; when we began our march towards Lundi Khana, and as we are well upon our way I will introduce a few verses which were composed by a Private of the 12th Regiment, entitled—

The Heroes of Afghanistan.

What is it makes our native land so high among the rest,
  How is it that her boundaries extend from east to west.
'Tis her Army small 'gainst fearful odds does always clear the way,
  And makes all rival nations feel the power of British sway.
And now to you I'll introduce each gallant British corps,   [war.
  Who shared the hardships, toil, and strife throughout the Afghan
And I am sure that when once more they cross the raging main,
  They will an hearty welcome find in England once again.
First on the list and in the field a corps to you I'll name,
  The 4th Brigade of Rifles, who wear the badge of fame.
Of statue short, and uniform as dark as clouds of night,   [height.
  They showed the Afghan Troops the way to climb each mountain

The 17th East Leicestershire come next upon the roll,
The "tiger" is their bold device, and is the pride of old.
O'er desert sands and burning plains of Egypt proud and bold,
And Ali Musjid's lofty heights, and Gundamuk so cold.

The 51st Light Infantry deserve our country's praise,
And when the Afghan war is known, their fame it will be raised.
The fierce Jowakies knew them and quickly felt them too,
And when they came the Afghan Hordes soon found enough to do.

Next comes the Lincoln Volunteers, the loyal 81st,
Who from Peshawar pressed forward, for martial fame athirst.
And though from fierce dysentry their numbers much declined,
(Which caused them shortly to return) they left their marks behind

And next to you I'll introduce, the gallant Fusiliers,
The Pride of old Northumberland for o'er two hundred years.
Exiled from fair Newcastles town, they did not care to pine,
But fought like men to win again, fresh honours for the Tyne.

The 25th Kings Borderers, next on the scene appear,   [fear.
And though their numbers were but few, they strangers were to
From duty's call their loyal hearts have never learned to swerve,
And for the way they played their part our hearty praise deserve.

The 8th of Kings we next observe, advancing to the fray,
With gallant spirits as of old, on many a well fought day.
Those hardy sons of Lancashire, well used to lives of toil,
Feared not to march o'er hills and dales, the Ameers plans to foil.

The Duke of Albany's Own Boys, the gallant Seventy 'twas,
Did next upon the scene appear, advancing to the wars,
Of statue tall and strong of limb, those sons of Scotland true,
Soon showed no savage Afghan tribe, could face their bonnets blue.

The 92nd Highlanders are the next we will review,   [true.
They bear the gallant Gordan name, and proved both staunch and
Their tartan plaid spread wide dismay, and caused the foe to reel,
The Afghan hordes could not withstand the force of Scottish steel.

The 59th Northamptonshire, I'll next describe to you,   [could do.
For when the Lilywhites were called they showed what they
And though for many years they'd served 'neath India's scorching
                                                            [sun,
They murmered not when duty called, they knew it must be
                                                        [done.

The gallant 12th I'll mention next ; we on their colours see,
  The Minden honors and not least, the Castle and the Key.
New Zealand did their prowess prove, as Englishmen well know,
  On Dhakka's lofty heights they laid, the savage Mohmunds low.

The 67th South Hampshire Boys were also in the field,   [weild.
  And proved true sons of Yoemen b ld, when called their guns to
If Afghan troops could stand the cold, why they could stand it too,
  And as for fighting thats a thing, they could much better do.

Next comes our Lancers bold and brave, old England's boast and
                                 [pride,
  And when the order came to charge they boldly in did ride.
Their Lances brightly gleaming, and poised high in the air,
  Which caused the foe the day to rue, they roused them from their
                                 [lair.

Those well trained mountain batteries have often caused a fright,
  To those wild tribes when they retire, to some secluded height.
For when they reach their mountain tops, they think themselves
                               [secure,
  Till kutcha guns into their midst, throw shells they can't endure.

But let us not forget to name the gallant Royal Horse,
  For when their guns begin to play, what can withstand their force.
Inside their forts the foe may seem, the British Power to dare,
  But soon a well directed shot will rout them from their lair.

The 10th Hussars winds up the list (the Prince of Wales' Own),
  Who on some future day may find a seat on England's throne.
Long may this true and gallant corps their honors live to wear,
  They did their duty at the front, and earned their laurels there.

And now to close my poem, whilst o'ft we praise our own,
  We'll not forget our Native troops, who well their share have done.
Those plucky little Goorkhas deserve our country's praise,
  The staunch Mhairwarris also helped our martial fame to raise.

The Bengal Lancers also claim a place among the brave,
  For many a time they nobly strove a hard fought field to save.
To each brave corps on this campaign, who nobly bore their part,
  Brittannia wishes all success, and thanks each gallant heart.

    Arriving at Lundi Khana we settled as before, and
next day continued our march to a place called Kata
Kooshtea. On the following morning we started off again,
passing through Ali Musjid, which though much improved

is still very unhealthy. The 39th Native Infantry who have
been stationed there during the last three months, having
lost nearly one hundred men by death and have at the
present time over half the regiment sick. On reaching
Shaghai heights we went into a standing camp, which saved
us the trouble of pitching our tents. During the night many
loosewalas came prowling round in search of plunder, but
the only thing they got was a good peppering from the
sentries. Early next morning the baggage escorted by a
strong guard, started off some time before the Regiment; but
had not got far down Makeson's road before about 200
Zukka Kheyls pounced down upon the hackeries with the
intention of looting them. They soon found out they had
made a mistake, for the baggage guard very quickly pounced
on them, and in a short time about a dozen of these robbers
were lying on the broad of their backs with bullet holes
through them, which showed that our men had shot pretty
straight. As soon as these men were killed the remainder
of the thieves took to flight, carrying of with them an old
pair of commissariat scales, which will do for them to
weigh the results of their foolish expedition. This was our
last bout with the Afghans and as usual it was a successful
one. A similar attack was made the day before on the
9th Lancers, and as their transport was very badly
guarded a large portion of the Officers' baggage was stolen
before the robbers were driven off. As they were successful
on this occasion they thought they would try the same game
with the gallant 5th, but as has been seen it completely
failed. Continuing our march down the pass, in a few hours
we had left Afghanistan behind and were snugly encamped
at Hurri Singh, and glad we were to be so, for the road all
the way we had come was lined with the rotting carcasses
of dead transport animals, the stench from which at times
was something dreadful. It is said that over 50,000 camels
have been lost since the commencement of the war, and this
I believe is quite true. Leaving Hurri Singh again next
morning we marched straight through Peshawar, and con-

tinued our journey until we had gone about five miles past the fort, when we pitched our tents at a place called Garra De Seer. Here we halted for a day to allow the two Companies from Markob and Bari Kab to join us. The two Companies having joined we started off again on the morning of the 11th, marching day after day until we arrived at Hussan Abdul. The march this far has been extremely fatiguing on account of the intense heat, which at times was over 130° in the tents. I am sorry to say we lost many men on the road from cholera, and as no coffins could be procured for their bodies they were each sewn up in a blanket and buried near the road side with nothing but a stone to mark their graves. Before I proceed any further, I will bring forward a poem which was composed by Sergeant Hoolihan, entitled—

THE DEATH MARCH OF THE BRITISH FROM AFGHANISTAN, A. D. 1879.

The Afghan hills resound no more,
   With trumpet blast or battle's roar ;
Backward the red hot march it lies,
   Where many a brave heart pines and dies.

The treaty did the Russian puzzle,
   The wily Afghan it did muzzle ;
Then to fair India we'll return,
   Although the sun do scorch and burn.

Backwards from Gundamukh the cold,
   Scene of British valour bold ;
The glorious stand of thirty-nine,
   The pen of poet can ne'er define.

Jellalabad is on the trail,
   Monument of Gallant Sale.
Ghilzai hordes and Cabul's crew ;
   Could ne'er his gallant band subdue.

Basawal thou place of heat and sand,
　Fit emblem of a blood-stained land ;
The assassin and cholera haunt thy plain,
　And death appears with his spectral train.

A Soldier lies through the weary night,
　Waging with cholera a grim death-fight ;
Comrades endeavour to soothe his pain,
　But all their efforts are in vain.

Cease comrades, cease, my race is run,
　Jack will never see another sun ;
My children orphans in a foreign land,
　While their father lies 'neath the Afghan sand.

Forward from this cursed soil away,
　And on we march 'fore break of day ;
The weary Soldier's onwards tread,
　Amidst the homes of the silent dead.

Next Dhakka's plain it comes in sight,
　Scene of the savage Mohmund fight ;
Its marshy soil and burning sand,
　Shrouds some more of our gallant band.

On, on, past Lundi Khana we fly,
　To Ali Musjid's fortress high ;
Onwards through these dreary regions,
　Where once marched Macedonian legions.

By Mackeson's road at dead of night,
　Afredee clans we put to flight ;
There fire it opens fierce and hot,
　Still Britain's sons they waver not.

Their ghostly dead on our pathway lie,
　With faces upturned to the sky ;
Such lessons strike terror in the Afredee glen,
　And says lo ! beware of the British men.

The plague striken pass we clear at last,
  And Jumrood's fort is quickly passed ;
Onwards we press unto Peshawar,
  Where chill ague carries all before.

Fair British faces come to welcome and view,
  The marching ranks of the bold and true ;
For their kindly greeting we give them thanks,
  And British cheers ring from the ranks.

On, past Nowshera we quickly glide,
  There the Cabul river flows swift and wide ;
Nowshera I like not thy hills of sand,
  Ah ! no I would seek a fairer land,

Fell cholera follows where'er we go,
  Will we never shake off this cursed foe ;
He revels and riots in his deathly pranks,
  And old comrades faces we miss from the ranks

Lo ! now we see Attock's forbidden river,
  Whose bridge of boats up-heave and quiver ;
There still I do not care to wonder,
  Though visions float o'er me of Alexander.

Hail ! Hussan Abdul to they groves and brook,
  The favoured haunt of fair Lalla Rookh ;
Where young Feramorz his tales he told her,
  A haven of rest finds the weary Soldier.

The crystal wells our frames revive,
  Where golden fishes sport and dive ;
If my heart in Albion did not lie,
  In thy calm sweet groves I could live and die.

For departed comrades now a prayer,
  Calm may they sleep they're free from care ;
The Khyber clans will be awed by each grave,
  For they know, beneath lies the silent brave.

My poem must end like the longest day,
  Who would envy the warrior his pay ;
Others are caressed and calmly sleep
  While the Soldier weary vigils keep.

Far away cross the ocean's width,
  Britain will remember the march of death ;
Orphans and widows she'll ne'er let repine,
  Whose guardians fell in seventy-nine.

Now off to Albion, the land of the free,
  Lo! I greet you fair isle of the sea ;
Strange lands I wish to see no more,
  But calmly rest on my native shore.

Leaving Hussan Abdul next morning, we left the grand
trunk road and turned to the left, continuing our journey
along the Cashmere road ; and as we are now marching
over ground which is new to us, I will give a slight description of our halting places as we come to them. Our first
camp was at Deyhar. There is not much to be seen here
except a large native village. Our next halt was at Hurripore, which is a good sized city, containing some very large
bazars. There are also some very fine orchards near, which
are filled with fruit trees of all kinds. Our next march was
to Sultanpore, which is not much of a place itself, but is
surrounded by very fine scenery. Next morning we
marched to Abbottabad, which is a beautiful place, full of
fine trees. A splendid little English church stands near
the centre of it, which puts one in mind of the country
villages at home. We pitched our tents in rear of the
cantonments, on a nice grassy piece of ground which was
as level and as well kept as a gentlemen's lawn. We now
thought we were rid of that foul disease cholera, but
unfortunately during the two days we stayed there several
fresh cases occurred : all of which, I am sorry to say, proved
fatal. Two of these cases were very lamentable indeed.
On the evening of the 22nd a man named Bodycott took

the disease, and was at once carried to the cholera tent. His brother who had gone to attend him was also stricken down shortly afterwards, and within a few hours both of them were dead, and next morning they were buried side by side. Both of them were fine looking men, and were much respected by their comrades. Not a single case had occurred in Abbottabad before our arrival, but before we had been there very long many cases took place among the inhabitants. A European resident wrote an indignant letter to the *Poineer* a few days afterwards, in which he says:

"Sir,—The 5th Fusiliers arrived at Abbottabad a few days ago, en route to their new hill station. Instead of encamping on open ground, this Regiment, fresh from the " cholera wave," pitched their tents on the parade ground of the 6th Punjab Infantry in a low situation, and almost in the midst of the cantonments. Instantly streets and bazaars were swarming with Soldiers and camp-followers, carrying infection wherever they went. What was the consequence : cholera immediately broke out where not a single case had before existed ; and Abbottabad is now having its turn of this frightful complaint. Who the gentlemen were who thrust the Regiment down into the midst of a town, I know not. But I do know that the whole land, with plenty of water, was before them to choose a suitable encamping ground as they pleased."

Leaving Abbottabad early on the 23rd we marched about 3 miles down the Cashmere Road and encamped on a piece of high ground near the small village of Chungi. Here we remained over a month while a road was being made to the top of a large hill, about 10 miles away, called Cheriala, which was a place where no troops had ever been before, and which was to be our station for the remainder of the summer, *i. e.* for the rains. It seemed rather late in the day to be only making a road to a place 6,000 feet above the sea, a place too which has yet to be cleared for camping on. During our stay in Chungi we had a deal of wet weather, which was the cause of much fever and dysentry; and I am sorry to say we had another attack of cholera which carried off several men. On July 28th, 2 companies left for Cheriala, being followed a day or two afterwards by 2 more, the remainder of the regiment following later on. These companies worked for many days, cutting down the trees which grew very thickly, and levelling the ground to pitch the tent upon; and as it rained most of the time they had a very hard time of it. After a while the top of the hill was pretty well cleared; but as there was only room enough for head-quarters, 4 companies, and the Regimental Hospital, the remaining compaines encamped about 2 miles lower down at a place called Lassatahai. By this time the rainy season had set in in full earnest, and while it lasted there was a great deal of sickness in the regiment. At one time there was nearly 300 men suffering from fever and dysentry; and besides this we lost several men from colic, which is a disease almost as fatal as cholera. All the other British Regiments that had returned from the front, had either gone into barracks, or to ready-made hill stations, where they had nothing to do but pitch their tents and rest quietly for the summer. The Old and Bold being the only Regiment that had to make a station for themselves, and as most of the men were pretty well knocked up by the hardships of the last ten months, this had not been so easily accomplished. Many men grumbled at the way they had been treated; but as it is a Soldier's duty to obey orders and not grumble, we made the best of it and settled down in our new station as comfortably as possible. As we are likely to remain here till November, I will bring this account of what "The Fusiliers Did " to a speedy close. Our losses from all causes during the campaign and the return march, was seventy of all ranks, and though these losses are bad enough, still they are not so severe as those suffered by several other corps. The 10th Hussars lost nearly half their regiment The 4th Battalion Rifle Brigade, 136 men. The 12th Regiment, 96. The 17th and 51st Regiments also losing many men. But the greatest losses of all fell to the lot of some of the Native Regiments, many of them suffering terribly. We all deeply regret the loss of so many brave men, and often miss many an old comrade's face from the ranks. The names of our officers and men who died, are as follows.

LIEUTENANTS.	J. FLETCHER.	T. CORBETT.
	A. HORNE.	J. JAMIESON.
J. G. OGLE.	S. CUTHBERT.	J. MURRAY.
A. C. GODWIN.	J. ELLISTON.	H. QUINN.
	G. ALLEN.	J. FONEY.
SERGEANTS.	J. HOOK.	T. SHABELSKIE.
	G. WOODS.	W. BROWN.
J. DONOUGHUE.	C. GRAY.	R. MORTON.
G. HARMER.	P. HEHEIR.	J. JAGGARD.
T. LAING.	W ASHTON.	S. COLLINS.
J. BIRD.	J. TOWNLEY.	R. COE.
	H. MILLWARD.	P. SHELDRAKE.
CORPORALS.	E. STRICKLAND.	J. COX.
	G. HEYBOURNE.	J. DOHERTY.
J. HINNIGAN.	M. WALSH.	E. FLETCHER.
J. McMANUS.	J. BROWN.	T. BAIN.
J. TIFFIN.	E. RUDD.	N. HENDERSON.
C. VALTINE.	W. TEAKLE.	T. HOOD.
J. RINGROSE.	J. HURLEY.	J. KEMP.
	F. PICKERING.	W. CARROLL.
LANCE CORPO-	G. ROBINSON.	W. McKENSIE.
RALS.	W. MORGAN.	J. NICOL.
	W. BODYCOTT.	J. BARRATT.
G. BODYCOTT.	J. FISHER.	J. McCABE.
J. TIMLIN.	J. WILSON.	J. MORAN.
W. DAVAY.	W. BARRETT.	
	J. ALDONS.	*APOTHECARY.*
PRIVATES.	J. COLE.	
	J. CARROLL.	W. KETTON.
J. SIMMONS.		

Our comrades who died numbered three-score and ten ;
All of them were good men and true ;
Respected by us who had known them so long,
And their untimely deaths we all rue.

'Tis sad for to think that so many brave men
  Should be taken while life's at its prime,
From the sides of their comrades who liked them so well,
  And laid 'neath the sod ere their time.

But wars and diseases their victims will have,
  And no one on earth can say nay ;
No man can prevent the cold hand of grim death
  From taking his comrades away.

How many poor mothers in England to-day
  Are weeping for sons that are slain ;
Who in happier times, were their hearts' joy and pride,
  But on earth whom they'll ne'er see again.

How many fond sisters are grieving as well
  For brothers whose spirits have fled ;
Who in childhood shared with them their sorrows and joys,
  But, alas ! who are now with the dead.

May these mothers and sisters that mourn now at home
  For brothers and sons in the grave,
Be consoled with the thought that like brave men they died
  The honour of England to save.

Ye men of the 5th that are living and well,
  I ask you now, every one,
That throughout your lives you will never forget,
  Your comrades of old that are gone·

May their faces and names on your minds be engraved,
  May you ever remember each man,
Who fell mid the battle or from foul disease,
  In the campaign in Afghanistan.

Her Majesty the Queen in her speech from the throne,
on August 16th, said : A Treaty has been concluded with the
Afghan Ameer, Yacoob Khan, which has happily terminated
the war which his predecessor, the late Ameer Sher Ali,
compelled my undertaking. Friendly relations are thereby
established, guarantees for peace and safety given, and the
Frontiers of my Indian Empire strengthened. The ability
of my Commanders, and the gallantry and endurance of
my Troops, deserved well the thanks of their country and
Parliament.

Ere I close let me say a few words for all those
  Of the 5th who went through the late war.
For our country we each one and all did our best,
  And what other troops could do more.

The cold of the mountains, the heat of the plains,
  We stood as true Britons should do.
And large and wide rivers, nigh up to our waists,
  We often times had to wade through.

By terrible hot winds we oft were assailed,
  And sand storms that darkened the skies.
And for months were tormented by merciless plagues,
  Of mosquitoes, snakes, ants, fleas, and flies.

Round our camps many thousands of camels lay dead,
  And the festering bodies of these
Spread among us (and many brave men were attacked)
  A foul and most deadly desease.

In front of the Afghans, our treacherous foes,
  We stood firm throughout the campaign,
And faced swords and bullets and fought them like men ;
  And if wanted, could do so again.

But now I will bring this account to an end,
  For I think I have said quite enough
To show that the 5th Fusiliers are made,
  Of the right sort of bold British stuff.

What the men of our gallant old regiment can do,
  Has many times over been seen.
We always are ready and willing to fight
  For Old England, and Old England's Queen.

END OF PART THE FIRST.

PART THE SECOND.

At the commencement of September an order was received to the effect that the regiment was to embark for England during the ensuing trooping season. This was good news to the majority of the men who were anxious to get home after being so many years in India. But this was not to be, for a few days afterwards the order was cancelled, and the 5th were doomed to remain another twelve months in the country. The cause of this was a very sad occurance which had occurred at Cabul. Major (now Sir Louis) Cavagnari and all his escort had been foully massacred. It seems that on September 3rd, five of the Ameer's regiments, which had just come to Cabul from Herat, broke out into open mutiny, and demanded from Douad Shah, their Commander-in-Chief, six months' pay which was due to them : he refused to pay them, saying he had not sufficient money to do so ; but offered to give them two months' pay there and then, and the remainder as soon as he could. This offer was refused by the mutineers with scorn, and several of them thinking the British Envoy was the cause of their demands not being satisfied, at once raised a cry of " let us kill the Kafirs." This cry was immediately taken up by the whole of the five regiments, who instantly rushed off to the Ameer's Arsenal, and returned in a few minutes armed to the teeth, bringing with them several large guns. They at once commenced to attack the residency which was defended so courageously by the Envoy and his escort (who numbered less than eighty) that three days elapsed before they had taken it, and then not till nearly the whole of its brave defenders had been killed, only two or three Native Soldiers escaping to tell the sad tale. This massacre put an end to all friendly relations with the Ameer, and a war of revenge was at once declared. On the 9th the regiment was warned for active service, but for some reason we still remained in Cheriala for several weeks. On October 21st, two companies were ordered to proceed to Kohat, and on the 28th they commenced their journey. As they are going to a place where none of our regiments have been before, we will accompany them to their destination.

Leaving Cheriala the two companies marched to Abbottabad, and stayed there till November 1st, when they proceeded to Sultanpore: leaving again next morning for Hurripore. On the following day they turned to the left, and marched along a very bad road (for the most part composed of dried up river beds) to a place called Huttar, where they encamped for the day. There was nothing much to be seen here except a native village and a large serai. Leaving Huttar next day, they continued marching for several miles, when they came out on the grand trunk road near General Nicholson's monument. Journeying for three miles further they then arrived at Janee ka Singh, where they halted. They left Janee ka Singh next moring and marched for several miles down the trunk road, and then turned to the right along the Kohat road. In an hour or so they were snugly encamped at Nawgazie, which is a place similar to Huttar. The next day's march was to Futteegungh, which is a good sized place containing a fine dak bungalow and a large bazaar. Next morning they arrived at camp Gagan and pitched their tents. Nothing much was to be seen here, except a small colony of Hindoo gipsies, who were encamped under a number of very delapidated old tents. The two companies halted here for a day to rest the baggage animals, and on the morning of the 9th proceeded to Ramilpore, where hardly anthying was to be seen but the bare camp ground. Next day they marched to Pindee Sultanee, which is a very nice place with a fine dak bungalow and a splendid camp ground. The next day's march was to Jhand where there are only a few mud huts and a dak bungalow. Leaving again next morning they journeyed along a very dusty road for about eight or nine miles, when they came to the River Indus, which at this place is rather narrow and flows between a cluster of large rocks. It is spanned as at Attock by a bridge of boats, which was so crowded with hackeries, camels, and a convoy of sick men returning from the Kurrum, that it was some time before our men could cross ; but at last they got over, and after marching a short distance further encamped at Kushalgurgh. They were now in what is called the Jowakie country, which at this spot looks very bleak and wild. Here they had to halt two days awaiting the arrival of E.-3., Royal Artillery, from Campbellpore, which they were to escort to Kohat. The Battery having arrived on the morning of the 15th (30 men having been told off to escort the guns), the whole of them marched to Goombat, which contains nothing much beyond a couple of large serais. Leaving early next morning they started for Kohat, and after marching 15 miles were met by the Bands of the 1st Madrassees and 1st Sikhs, who played them to a very large bungalow, which was to be their quarters. The men having halted and the Bands stopped playing, the whole of them were shortly afterwards marched into the bungalow, which was quite bare, there being nothing in it but a few old native charpoys. The Artillery men took up one half the bungalow and our men the other half, and all proceeded to settle down as quickly and as comfortably as they could ; and now we will leave them for a short time while I give a slight description of the station. Kohat is near the entrance of the Kurram Valley, and was until the signing of the Treaty of Gundamuck one of the Chief Frontier Stations. There are many fine roads in it, the sides of them being lined with large trees, among which many grape vines and banana trees are to be seen. Many fine streams run through different parts of the station ; but although the water is bright and sparkling to look at, it is impregnated with saltpetre, and cannot be drank until it has been filtered. There is a splendid dak bungalow, a good sized post office, a beautiful little English church, and many fine looking gentlemen's bungalows. Besides these there are several large barracks and a couple of well kept parade grounds, which are more like parks than anything else. But I think the most interesting place in Kohat is the fort, which though small, is a model one, and complete in every way. It stands on a fine piece of ground, and commands the entrance of the Kurram Valley. A short distance from the fort is the native city, which is very large, and is almost as famous for its crimes as the city of Peshawar. Its bazaars are daily crowded with the most ruffianly looking set of beings that it has ever been my lot to gaze upon. There are Afghans, Kohistanis, Tartars, Persians, and hillmen of every description, and it requires a large number of well armed Native police to keep them in order. Many murders are committed here, and a large gallows (capable of hanging two men at a time) which stands just outside the gates, is often required to carry out the law of a life for a life, &c. The two companies being pretty well settled in their new quarters, we will now leave them and see what has been going on at head-quarters in the meantime. Three days after the two companies left Cheriala for Kohat head-quarters and the remainder began to leave Cheriala and Sassatahai, one or two companies at a time, and by the 10th of November the whole of them were encamped at Abbottabad. On the 14th the regiment left and marched to Sultanpore; on the 15th to Hurripore; 16th to Deyhar; and on the 17th to Hussan Abdul. Here they were ordered to wait for further orders. On the 22nd a number of men joined the regiment from the depôt at Chakrata. On December 16th, the regiment was ordered to proceed to Peshawar, and next morning commenced its march, encamping for the day at Huttee. The next day's march was towards the Indus, which the regiment crossed, and pitched their tents at Khyrabad. In the afternoon orders came for the regiment to be in Peshawar on the 20th. This being the 18th, and Peshawar over 50 miles away, of course there was nothing left for it but to do two forced marches. Accordingly next morning the first one was commenced. On arriving at Nowshera our men were agreeably surprised to see the roadside near the barracks, lined with large tables piled up with bread and cheese, and huge cans of beer, which the men of the 17th had provided for them as a return for the kindness they had received from our regiment in Basawal, on their return from the Dea Surak expedition. Our men having already marched over 18 miles, they were naturally very hungry and thirsty, and did full justice to these good things, I can assure you. When every one had had their fill, the regiment was ordered to fall in again, and after thanking the 17th for their great kindness, and vowing everlasting friendship towards them, left Nowshera, and marched 3 miles further to Turseil, and encamped for the day. Early the following morning the regiment left for Peshawar, and after a very dusty and fatiguing march they arrived there and went straight into barracks. On the 23rd an order came for one company of the regiment to proceed to Lundi Kotal on convoy duty next day. Accordingly next morning the first company of the 5th Fusiliers to go to Afghanistan during the present campaign, started off towards Jumrood, escorting a convoy of treasure, amunition, and stores. On arriving at Jumrood they pitched their tents and remained there for the night; next morning, December 25th, they left for Ali Musjid. This was Christmas day and a very miserable one it was, rain and hail pouring down nearly the whole of the day. On account of the wet and slippery nature of the road, and the slowness of the convoy they were escorting, the company did not reach Ali Musjid till very late. This place has greatly altered since the regiment marched down last June, and many improvements have taken place, the most notable one being the new fort, which has been erected on the same spot where the old one stood. It has a very strong and well built look about it, and should be able to withstand any attack that might be made upon it. To any one gazing up at it from the camp it looks quite grand, with its loopholed sides and fine bastions, from one of which floats that dear old flag, The Union Jack. The flag that's braved the battle and the breeze for many a long year, and for the honour of which every true Briton is ready to fight to the death.

Its only a small bit of bunting, only an old coloured rag,
  Yet thousands have died for its honour, and shed their best blood
    for the flag.
I'ts charged with the Cross of Saint Andrew, which of Old Scotland's
  heroes has led,
  It carries the Cross of Saint Patrick, for which Ireland's bravest
    have bled.

Joined with these is our own English Ensign, Saint George's Red
  Cross on white field,
  Round which from King Richard to Wolsley, Britons conquered
    but never did yield.
It floats o'er the ocean triumphant, as free as the wind and the
  wave,
  And the bandsman from shackles unloosened 'neath its shadow
    no longer's a slave.

It flutters o'er Malta and Cyprus, over Canada, India, Hong Kong,
  And Britons where'er their flag's flying, claim the rights that to
    Britons belong.
We hoist it to show our devotion to our Queen, to our country,
  and laws,
  Its the outward and visible emblem of advancement and liberty's
    cause.

You may call it an old bit of bunting, you may say its an old
  coloured rag.
  But freedom has made it majestic, and time has enobled the
    flag.

Leaving Ali Musjid next day, the Company journeyed to Lundi Kotal where they were ordered to remain till further orders. On the 29th another Company left Peshawar and escorted I.-C. Battery, Royal Horse Artillery, to Lundi Kotal, where they arrived on the 31st. On January 4th the two companies that had been on detachment in Kohat, rejoined head-quarters in Peshawar. Having been relieved in Kohat by two companies of the Rifle Brigade. On the 8th two more companies of the fifth left Peshawar and did a forced march to Ali Musjid, and next day continued their journey to Lundi Kotal, where they joined the companies already there. On the 10th Douad Shah, the Afghan Commander-in-Chief (who had been made a prisoner by

General Roberts at Cabul), was brought into Lundi Kotal by a squadron of the 6th Carabineers. Next day he was sent to Jumrood, being escorted about half way to Ali Musjid by a number of the 5th Fusiliers, where he was taken over by other troops. As it was thought that the tribesmen might attempt to rescue him in the narrow and difficult parts of the pass between Ali Musjid and Jumrood, a flying column about 1,000 strong, of which 250 of the 5th Fusiliers formed part, was sent from Peshawar to Jumrood as a precautionary measure. This column returned again to Peshawar next day and encamped near the barracks. On the following morning, January 13th, it marched to Fort Michni, which is about 8 or 10 miles to the right of Jumrood. The reason of it being sent here was because the Mohmunds were in arms, and it was feared they might attempt to invade British territory in these parts. The flying column was ordered to remain round about Fort Michni, until the return of an expedition which was to be sent against the Mohmunds on the 15th. During the past fortnight many rumours have been abroad at Lundi Kotal, to the effect that the Mohmunds were collecting their forces to invade British territory, and these rumours have at last been verified. Various causes have been assigned for the new jehad, the prinicipal one being that Yacoob Khan's mother being a Mohmund, her kinsmen would not allow her to be taken to India without attempting a rescue. Another, and a more propable reason being, that this particular tribal rising merely forms a part of the grand combination inaugurated by Mahomed Jan in the vicinity of Cabul. However, be that as it may, it is now quite certain that these Mohmunds intended to give us some trouble. When all doubt as to the enemy's intentions had been set at rest, and our spies had made it certain that large numbers were in the act of crossing to this, the right or southern bank of the Cabul river, it was decided to attack them as soon as possible ; accordingly early on the morning of the 15th a force left Lundi Kotal for this purpose. It was composed of 200 of the 5th Fusiliers, under Major Taylor ; 200 of the 25th regiment, 300, 31st Punjabies; 200, 4th Madrassees; 300, 1st Madrassees; 1 Troop Bengal Cavalry; 1 Company Native Sappers, and 2 Mountain guns. In all some 1,300 men, under the immediate command of General Doran. At the same time as this column started another column of about the same strength, under Colonll Boisragon, also left Dhakka Fort with the intention of co-operating. The enemy being known to occupy in great force the Gara hills which overhang the village of Dhakka, as also the intervening strip of country between these hills and Kam Dhakka, it was resolved if possible, to entangle them by the 2 columns closing in, so that the only escape for the Mohmunds could be by recrossing the river, which would be under any circumstances a tedious and difficult operation for a large body of men, more especially when the only available means were mussacks, with an odd raft or two. The Lundi Kotal column proceeded up the Logari Valley in a northernly direction for about 2 miles, when striking westwards it reached the Kotal, connecting Torsuppa and Angjir ke Jawar. Here a halt was made to allow the rear of the column to close up. Shortly afterwards the descent into the Suleiman Valley was commenced. The road was extremely bad and progress very slow, the water and ammunition mules frequently coming to grief, so much so that the halts became numerous. This mountain path, however, had an immense advantage over the one taken by Colonel Norman's force on a somewhat similar occasion last April, as it saved about eight miles—an all important point when a surprise was intended. After a time the ground became more open, and when the Anjiri ke Jawar spur had been cleared, the force discovered the enemy posted on the Suleiman Gakka heights, a huge red banner being a conspicuous object. The disposition for the attack was quickly made. The ground to be covered consisted of stony open pieces, with a series of open pieces running at right angles to the enemy's position. The 5th Fusiliers formed on the right, and the men of the 25th regiment on the left, with the mountain guns in the rear covered by a company of Native Infantry, while the supports consisted of the 31st Punjabies and the 1st Madrassees, the advance was then ordered. When the second ridge had been reached, the mountain guns opened fire, dropping a few shells with great precision into a sungar filled with armed men. The Infantry also fired a few volleys but without doing much execution owing to the long range; a further advance was then ordered, when the force reached the head of the long defile which debouches on Kam Dhakka, the objective point of the movement. The men of the 25th regiment taking the left of the defile, and the 5th Fusiliers the right: the task of clearing the heights naturally devolved upon the latter corps, and looking at the position from below it seemed a task of no mean difficulty. The 5th Fusiliers did the business in a very efficient manner; and in less than half an hour from the time of commencing their climb, had gained the crest and sungars of the enemy's position. The Mohmunds conti- nued their fire on the attacking party, till they had got within one hundred yards; but shot wildly, and as a rule too high. Only one of our men was struck, although of course there was any number of close shaves. The volleys of the covering parties was so close and well directed as to prevent the enemy doing any serious dam- age. The estimated number of the Mohmunds at this point was about 500, and had they defended their enormously strong position with the most ordinary pluck, they must have made it extremely hot for the men of the 5th, who numbered little over 120 men; and in addition to carrying accoutrements and 70 rounds of ammunition, had to climb a most precipitous hill. On gaining the position the enemy were seen scuttling up the hills on the opposite side of the interposing ravine, and the men of the 5th by volley firing brought down about a score of them in addition to any loss that might have been previously inflicted. The position was occupied at 2 p.m., and from thence large bodies of men could be seen descending the right bank of the Cabul river. As the right flank was now clear, all the troops were recalled from the Suleiman Gakka heights, and the descent towards the river began. After a toilsome and weary trudge, the head of the column reached the end of the Gakka gorge, as it debouched on the Cabul river. About 2,000 of the enemy being discovered, some 800 yards down stream, in the act of crossing or having crossed, the mountain guns and 2 companies of European Infantry were got quickly into position, when some vigorous shelling, and rattling volleys of musketry, was kept up on the retiring masses for fully 20 minutes. A raft containing some 200 was a conspicuous object to aim at, and judging by the numbers seen to fall, a loss of over 30 must have been inflicted. As evening was now closing in, and the enemy were well out of range, a a move was made for Kam Dhakka, about a quarter of a mile up stream, where the column from Dhakka arrived about the same time, having well performed their share of the programme. Marching from Fort Dhakka they soon cleared the Gara hills of all opposition, the Horse Artillery guns making beautiful practice, dropping shells into sungars with the utmost precision. The Infantry then scaled the heights, and by 2 p. m. all resistance had ceased. The 2 columns bivouacked for the night near the village of Kam Dhakka, and for the Lundi Kotal column it was a cold and cheerless one. No baggage had turned up, and the men had neither blankets nor great coats, food was scarce and it froze hard. About 10 p. m. some 20 men who had been hiding near the village, made a bolt of it up the gorge in rear, and were at once fired upon by the picquets, with what result is unknown. Beyond this temporary alarm the night passed quietly. Next day, the 16th, it was placed beyond doubt that the right bank of the river had been entirely cleared of the Mohmunds. On the following day 500 men of the Dhakka column crossed the river on rafts, and occupied the large village of Reina, where they bivouacked for the night, and next day (the 18th) set the place in flames, and blew up a very large tower which was a conspicuous object from the opposite shore, recrossing the river again shortly afterwards. Meanwhile the Lundi Kotal column had cleared out, making straight for Haftchah, by an unfrequented path at the back of the Gara heights, and reached camp the same day. A party of the 4th Madrassees who had performed the thankless duties of baggage guard, had been for 3 days stuck in the Suleiman Gakka Pass, and by almost superhuman efforts at last succeeded in getting everything into camp. The casualties on our side, was one killed and eight wounded, and that of the Mohmunds has been estimated at 200 killed and wounded. So ended an invasion that at first threatened serious consequences, not so much from the character and number of the invaders, as from the small body of troops at our disposal (at one time), too small to send a flying column to meet them. That the blow inflicted on the Mohmunds was not as complete or severe as it might have been, is an undoubted fact; still the operations were a success, and the moral effect of our being able to cross the river under their eyes, and burn one of their largest villages, will be such as to think twice before troubling us again. On the same day as the troops returned from the expedition just narrated, the 18th, the flying column sent out from Peshawar to Fort Michni (not having seen any signs of the Mohmunds near that place), returned again to Peshawar, where it was broken up: the troops rejoining their several regiments. On the 22nd headquarters and the remaining companies of the 5th Fusiliers left Peshawar and marched to Lundi Kotal, where they arrived on the 24th. On the 25th one company of the regiment proceeded on detachment to Fort Dhakka; and on February 2nd, 2 more companies marched to Basawal and took up their quarters in the Fort. During the next 2 months things went along very quiet round about Lundi Kotal; but at the same time the men had enough to do, doing guards, pickets, convoy duty, escorting guns, &c. The weather during this time was bitterly cold, and it was as much as the troops could do to keep themselves warm. On April 9th, Her Majesty's 14th Regiment marched into Lundi Kotal to relieve the 5th Fusiliers, who were ordered to

Pesh Bolak. On the following day, the 5th were ordered to change camps with the 14th, but owing to the wetness of the weather, this was not done until the 12th. On the 13th the regiment left Lundi Kotal and marched to Dhakka, where we were joined by the company that had been on detachment in the Fort. Our march next day was to Basawal, where we pitched our tents almost on the same spot as we had occupied 12 months before. On the morning of the 16th the Regiment left Basawal, being shortly afterwards followed by the 2 companies from the Fort. After marching for 7 or 8 miles over very rough and stony ground, we halted and pitched our tents on a nice clean piece of ground near the friendly village of Pesh Bolak. For several days every available man was hard at work, building breastworks and other fortications round about the camp, so as to be prepared for any enemy who might venture to attack us. On the 23rd we were joined by about 20 men who had come from Chackrata, Rawal Pindee, and Peshawar. As this was Saint George's day (the second we had spent in · Afghanistan) of course we could not let it pass without celebrating it in some way or other. In the afternoon each man was served out with an extra and free dram of rum, and in the evening we had an open air concert, the programme of which consisted of singing, dancing, and selections by the Band. The singing was very good indeed, and so was the clog dancing; but unfortunately the clogs were in Europe and boots had to be used in their stead. The selections by the Band were extremely well played, and every man who was lucky enough to be present, passed a most enjoyable evening. On the 26th the regiment was ordered to proceed to Safed Sang, as soon as the 14th Regiment from Lundi Kotal should relieve us. This order was good news to us all, as we were anxious to go further up the country. During our stay here the people round about have been very quiet indeed, not a shot having been fired since we came. Although Dea Surak, where the chief villages of the Shinwarris (whom we severely punished last year, and who are still hostile to us) are located is only about 3 miles away, these fierce tribesmen have given us no trouble so far. The reason of this is, I suppose on account of the fine moonlight nights we have had lately. The month of May has come, and we are still here, the 14th not having yet arrived; but we are expecting them them every day, and when they do come they will come into a warm place and no mistake. Although Pesh Bolak is not so much subject to plagues of flies and foul smells as Basawal, still it is extremely hot, and is often visited by hot winds and dust storms.

An officer, a day or two ago, in a letter to the *Pioneer* says : Sir,—I saw in the *Pioneer*, some days since, some remarks as to the excessive heat at Basawal and other places on the Khyber line. Would you be surprised to hear that the thermometer now stands here in Pesh Bolak at 114˙ in the tents. Such is the case, and yet this delightful spot was selected, after a tremendous amount of hesitation and discussion, as a sanitarium to avoid the heat and dust of Basawal. I do not know much about Basawal, but I believe there is supposed to be only a thin sheet of paper between it and another place, and I fancy Pesh Bolak must run Basawal very close both as regards heat and dust.

To sit in dust, eat, drink and breathe it as well,
To search in vain for some bright spot of green,
Where men that own not our dominion dwell,
And Christian foot hath ne'r or rarely been.

To climb a trackless hill and vent one's spleen
On bobbery mules by drivers uncontroll'd
Gainst shrivelled trees and blazing rock to lean,
This is not soldiering, tis but to hold
Converse with Satan's charms, and see his stores unroll'd.

On May 5th, at 5 a. m., we left Pesh Bolak and marched to Elatchipore. For about five miles our route lay over very rough ground, all ups and downs, and covered with stones of all sizes. After going this distance we came out on the old main road, where about a mile down we could see the 14th Regiment on their march from Basawal to Pesh Bolak. Crossing the main road we journeyed along a new road which had been made since we were up before. During the last six miles of our march we passed by several large villages, with the ground about them very well cultivated. On arriving at Elatchipore we pitched our tents near the Fort, which is a large one, garrisoned by Native Troops, and capable of making a good defence should it at any time be attacked. This day's march was an extremely hot one, each one of us on arrival being saturated with sweat, and the only wonder is that no one was attacked with heat apoplexy. Leaving again next morning, we marched in the direction of Ali Bogan. After going about a mile, the road turns slightly to the left, and runs for about six miles along the foot of some large hills near the Cabul river. It then gradually ascends the hill sides, for about two miles, when it attains the height of several hundred feet above the level of the river. The view from here is something to be remembered. On our left is the steep and rocky sides of wild and barren mountains, and on our right, on the other side of the river, is a beautiful valley, dotted here and there with villages surrounded by large trees and fields of ripe corn. The road from here commences to descend until it reaches a small plain, where about half a mile across, stands Fort Ali Bogan, which is something similar to the one at Elatchipore. Near this fort we pitched our tents and rested for the day. As nearly the whole of this day's march was under the shadow of the hills, and along the side of the Cabul river, it was much cooler than the one we did the day before. The night before we came, 3,700 Mohmunds crossed the river near here, with the intention of attacking the fort; but on being told by a friendly tribesman that the Kafirs (meaning in this instance the gallant 5th) were coming, they thinking discretion was the better part of valour, recrossed again and dispersed to their villages. Leaving Ali Bogan next morning, we marched down a road running across a very sandy plain, with a small stream here and there, until we came within half a mile of Jellalabad, when we passed a few trees and a small plot of cultivated ground. On arriving at our destination we pitched our tents just outside Fort Sale (so named after General Sale, the Jellalabad hero of 1841). This fort has only lately been built by our people. In shape it is square, with a thick mud wall running all around it. In each of the corners, stands a good sized bungalow, the walls of which are perforated by loopholes, so that they can be defended from the inside if attacked. Three of them are occupied by European Troops, the remaining one being used as an hospital. There is also accommodation for 500 or 600 Native Troops, and besides these there are several large sheds, filled with hundred of tons of ordnance and commissariat stores of all kinds. Altogether it seems to be a very strong, large and well built place, and the garrison at present within its walls, should be able to hold their own against all the Afghans that could be brought against them. In the evening an order came from Brigadier General Doran, that the 5th Fusiliers were to remain in Jellalabad until further orders. Between 10 and 11 p. m. there was a great deal of firing going on at the other side of the city, thinking it was the tribes fighting among themselves no notice was taken of it, but before many hours had elapsed it was found out that something quite different had occurred. About 3 a. m. news was brought to the Political Officer, in the Fort, that over 1,000 head of commissariat cattle which had been entrusted to the care of some friendly tribesmen, and which were located in a compound about two miles away, had been looted by a number of Ut Kheyl robbers from the Lughman Valley. It seemed rather curious that this news did not reach the authorities until four hours after the robbery had been committed, and it was strongly suspected that the so-called friendly tribesmen who had charge of the cattle, were in league with the robbers who stole them. This suspicion afterwards turned out to be correct. Although the robbers had got four hours' start, it was decided to send a force after them. The camp was at once aroused, and the 5th Fusiliers, accompanied by a number of Troopers of the Central Indian Horse, and several Afghan Guides, started in pursuit shortly afterwards. After leaving camp we marched along for a mile-and-half, when we reached the Peshawar gate of Jellalabad city, which we entered. Even at a time like this, it was impossible to pass through this gateway without thinking of the brave men who marched through it years ago, and fought Akbar Khan's army in the plain where our camp is now pitched, and completely destroyed his force ; and then a few months later Polock's avenging army marched through this same gateway, while the band of the 13th played " Aye, but ye've been lang a coming." Leaving the gateway we marched through the main street of the city, which was all in darkness and almost totally deserted. It was impossible to pass along it without imagining the scenes which took place here in 1841, when Sale and Havelock, with the brave men of the 13th, made this Afghan city illustrious in the annals of brave deeds, which have been recorded in the pages of history concerning our army. On reaching the end of the main street we passed out of the city by the Cabul gateway, which vividly brought to mind, that through this gateway Dr. Bryden, the only survivor of the Cabul army, rode in in an almost dying state from fatigue and starvation, to tell the sad sad story of the massacres in the Jugdullak Pass, the treacherous murders at Futteeabad, and the annihilation of Elphinstone's army. Leaving the city behind we marched along at a very quick rate, for several miles, over ground of all kinds; good, bad and indifferent. It was now broad daylight, and we passed by several patches of blood, which showed that the thieves must have goaded the poor animals dreadfully in their haste to get into the mountains, out of reach of the troops, who they well knew would be sent after them, as soon as the raid was found out. After wading through several streams, and marching a few miles further, we commenced to ascend a large hill, but had hardly reached the top before several shots were fired at us from an opposite hill, by a number of the robbers, who, no doubt, had remained behind, while their companions got away with the cattle. These shots were at once returned, and then commenced a lot of skirmishing among the hills, which lasted for an hour or two, during which time several of the robbers were seen to fall, their bodies being carried away by their comrades. As the sun was now very powerful and many of the men were showing signs of exhaustion, the force was ordered to retire; the Political Officer saying it was of no use following the robbers any further, as they had got too much of a start. As soon as we were well out of the hills again, we were halted and told to fall out for a while, when each of us was served out with half a pound of bread and some tinned meat, which with some water from the river, made us a very good meal. Having fell in again we started on our march towards camp. We got a good view of the city coming back. It seems to be about 2 miles in circumference, perfectly square in shape, and surrounded by a very high and thick mud wall, with bastions here and there for defence, and in many parts is in a very delapidated condition. The bazaars are very narrow and unspeakably filthy, the shops have an equally dirty appearance, and the men who squat in them are no cleaner. The only exception is the main bazaar, which is wider and is covered by a wooden roof slung from one side of the street to the other, as a protection against rain and the heat of the sun. It was in the height of business when we passed through, and was crowded with ruffianly looking Afghans of all descriptions, whose scowling countenances plainly told that their owners were anything but friendly towards us. Leaving the city we marched to camp, where we arrived about 5 p. m., wet and hungry, and pretty well tired out. Next morning a man named Miller was reported missing, and as he had not been in camp all night, it was thought he might have been shot in the hills the day before, and falling into some crevice in the rocks was passed by unnoticed. A number of friendly Afghans were at once sent out to search the hils. They searched all day, but could find no trace of him whatever. Continuing the search again next morning, they came across his body on one of the hills; it was stark naked, and nearly cut in two below the waist, and the head had been battered frightfully. None of his clothes, arms, or accoutrements were found. The body was brought into camp and was burried at dusk in the evening. The cattle raid was a very unlucky affair altogether, for the robbers not only managed to get clear away with the cattle, but the troops had a deal of hard marching for nothing, and this poor man Miller had lost his life.

I have several verses about this raid, which are supposed to have been composed, by a very gifted Moolah belonging to the same tribe as the raiders; they are as follows :—

Hoo, Allah, il Allah. Bismallah, be Islam, exalted and praised.
    And trebly accurst be the Kafir, his sisters, his cousins, his aunts,
I sing of a deed which but lately that hog-eating Kafir amazed,
    When a thousand sleek beeves, our great heroes brought back to
        their wild mountain haunts.
So gather ye sons of the Moslem, ye warriors elect of the lord,
    Sit round on your fragments of carpet, sit round your grey bard in a
        ring.
Make no interruption unseemly, but each feel the edge of his sword,
    And freely expectorate on them, in fancy the dogs, while I sing—

BARD CANIT.

Up tribesmen all, good news, good news : 'twas Robbuz Khan that
        spoke,
    One of the brave jezailchi band, who love their little joke.
Who in the service of our foes lip-service take their ease,
    And bag with much disdain the while the Kafir's vile rupees.
Good news, good news, cried Robbuz Khan, near yonder camp to
        night,
    A thousand goodly oxen rest, in sooth a glorious sight.
And I dont see, said Robbuz Khan, I'm sure no more do you,
    Now why we should not help our friends each to a byle or two.
For our vile foes, whose brains you know, are like the pigs they eat,
    Have placed them in our charge that we may give our friends a
        treat.

So spoke the doughty Robbuz Khan ; the news spread far and wide,
   And soon a trusty gathering of braves was at his side.
Their match-locks true, were primed and oiled, their knives were
   sharp and bright.
   And by Mahomed's beard they swore they'd loot the lot that night.
As so when evening's shades came down, these warriors came down
   too,
   And stealthily the camp approached, and much enjoyed the view.
For there nigh the Ameer his bagh, they joyfully espied
   One thousand byles in tranquil dose, and other loot beside.
They tarried not, but straightway drove those drowsy byles away,
   And helped themselves to other loot, and not did say them nay.
And merrily they laughed to think, that while the Kafir snored,
   They'd taken such precious loot, and one, undoubtedly, had scored.

      *   *   *   *

Oh ! when the sleepy Kafir woke, and rubbed his drowsy eye,
   And found his oxen gone, he called the ninety-forth N. I.
To arms, and stamped and swore, they say, and followed in their
   track,
   And vowed by all his gods, that he would die or have them back.
But sly old Rummun Khan, whose wit is known our valleys through,
   Told off to stand upon a hill, a trusty man or two.
Instructing each that when upon the plain appeared our foes,
   With fierce disdainful frown, to raise his fingers to his nose.'
So when the Kafir's troops appeared, each tribesman raised a shout,
   And placed his thumb against his nose and spread his fingers out.
And this defiant attitude, backed by a dropping fire,
   Soon caused the weak-kneed foe to turn, and hastily retire.

      *   *   *   *

Oh, merrily our sons shall tell, when years have glided by,
   The tale of how their fathers did the Kafir in the eye.
Still fierce and free they'll curse with one, the vile Feringi's vaunts,
   And pray may Allah blight him, and his cousins, and his aunts.

I think the Moolah who made these verses, composed
them rather too soon, for not only were the friendly tribesmen who had charge of the cattle fined 4,000 rupees, but a
force was sent out from Safed Sang which looted and destroyed the villages of the Utkhcyls, and recovered nearly the
whole of the cattle.   On May 11th, Kalu Khan, brother of the
Governor of Jellalabad, was out with a number of his
followers on the other side of the river, gathering revenue

for the British, when he came across a large village, the inhabitants of which not only refused to pay the taxes, but at once set about the tax gatherers, who were forced to retreat. Kalu Khan sent over for assistance, and as the Jellalabad people are great enemies of those across the river, the Governor asked permission to take over (in addition to his own followers) some of the city people, and this request being granted, he went over at once and joined his brother. The villagers again refused to pay the taxes and then commenced a tremendous row almost in sight of the camp, which ended in a victory for the tax gatherers: the villagers being thoroughly beaten and compelled to pay the revenue. On May 12th, 100 men of the 5th proceeded to Gundamukh, being followed on the 14th by 100 more, and two days afterwards by fifty more, escorting two guns of C-3, Royal Artillery. Their first march lay along a very bad road, almost a foot deep in sand, for about 14 miles when they came to Rosabad, which consists of a native village and a splendid fort, near which they encamped. The next day's march was along a pretty good road to Fort Battye, and the following day's march was pretty good for about half way, when the road began to ascend and continued all up hill until they arrived at Gundamuck, where they encamped; a few days afterwards 100 of these men marched into Fort Safed Sang where they had plenty of hard duty to perform. After the 250 men had left for Gundamuck, the remainder of the regiment was ordered to remain in Jellalabad, probably for the summer. The majority of the men did not much relish the idea of summering (simmering is a better word) under canvass in Jellalabad, which is during the hot season anything but a desirable place to remain in. On the 17th the 12th regiment came into Jellalabad: they were on their way to India, having been invalid on account of so many men being sick. On the same day two companies of the 5th marched into the fort, and relieved a detachment of the 12th who were ordered to join their regiment. Next morning a force, including head-quarters, and the remaining companies of the Fusiliers crossed the river, on an expedition against a tribe called the Safis. The account of this expedition cannot be better told than by giving the whole of Brigadier-General Doran's despatches, which are as follows :—

Dated Fort Sale, Jellalabad, 27th May 1880.

From—Brigadier-General J. DORAN, C. B., Commanding 2nd Section, Khyber Line Force,

To—The Deputy Adjutant General, Khyber Line Force, Safed Sang.

I have the honor to forward herewith an account of the recent military operations in Besud.

2. For some time past that district, lying on the left bank of the Kabul river, and directly opposite Jellalabad, had been threatened by a gathering of Safis and others under the leadership of Mullah Khalil, his following comprising men from the Dara-i-Nur and villages in the Kunar valley, north of Besud. The beginning of this movement was reported to you by telegram on the 9th instant, and, as I anticipated that the gathering might eventually have to be dispersed by force, I halted on that day the 5th Fusiliers, then on their march to Safed Sang. At the same time I directed that rafts should be prepared for the passage of the Kabul river, the bridges over the two northernmost branches having been carried away some time before.

3. On the 12th May I was informed by Major Protheroe, Political Officer at Jellalabad, that Mullah Khalil with 1,000 men, had arrived at Nargal, and contemplated a descent upon Besud so soon as he should have collected more followers to his standards. On the 13th May, I should have thrown a small force of infantry across the Kabul had rafts been ready. They were completed by the 14th, and that evening 200 bayonets of the 1st and 4th Madras Native Infantry crossed the river and occupied the Fort of Dabela, which had been placed at my disposal by the Khan of Jellalabad.

4. On the afternoon of the 15th, Major G. Tyndall, 1st Madras Native Infantry, commanding the troops in Besud, reconnoitred as far as Kalu Khan's Fort in view to reporting on the route our force would take. This report was forwarded to you. By this time Mullah Khalil's following was reported to be upwards of 1,200 strong, and to have reached Islampur. It was also stated that the people of Shewa, Shigi, and the neighbouring villages had expressed their intention of turning out to bar Mullah Khalil's way to the entrances into Besud by the Tukchi and Paikob Tangis. On this date, the 15th, I considered it advisable to cross some cavalry. That afternoon 55 sabres of the Central India Horse effected the passage by swimming across the northern branch of the Kabul, 150 yards wide at this point, and with a current of between five and six miles an hour. A separate report was sent you on this subject: here I need only say that 55 horses and 25 ponies swam the river, and, with all the baggage, saddlery, &c., of the troop, were in Besud within the hour, no casualty or even hitch having occurred.

5. On the 17th news was brought that the enemy had advanced to Kalatik, and had sent small parties to hold the Paikob and Tokchi Tangis. A cavalry reconnoissance that afternoon verified the latter report, our sowars being fired at from both *tangis*. They stated that the former was held by about 100 men, the latter by about 500, and that villagers in the neighbourhood had told them that 1,000 more of the enemy under Mullah Khalil had reached Shigi. On this day, the 17th, the 12th Foot arrived at Jellalabad *en route* to India, with two guns of No. 1 (Kohat) Mountain Battery for service. Being very short of infantry, I stopped the regiment.

6. On the morning of the 18th I sent the mountain guns and 200 of the 5th Fusiliers across the river, and that afternoon 200 of the 12th Foot—all that were available in that corps—and another troop of the Central India Horse. To-day, too, I learnt that the enemy might possibly number

four or five thousand men, and that we might have to take the fort of Abdul Khel, then held by them. Not considering the small force at my disposal equal to cope successfully with such numbers, probably holding a very strong position on the heights as well as the fort, I applied to the Major-General for five to six hundred more infantry. In reply I was told to attack next day.

7. Accordingly, next day, the 19th instant, having left a few men in Dabela Kila, I proceeded with No. 1 Mountain Battery, two Guns under Lieutenant F. R. Thackeray, R. A.; 1st Battalion 5th Fusiliers, 175 bayonets, under Lieut.-Colonel T. Rowland; 1st Battalion 12th Regiment, 183 bayonets, under Lieut.-Colonel C. J. C. Sillary; Central India Horse, 79 sabres, under Lieut.-Colonel C. Martin; 1st Madras Native Infantry, 92 bayonets, and 4th Madras Native Infantry, 92 bayonets, both under Major G. Tyndall, 1st Madras Native Infantry, to carry out my instructions. We left Dabela Kila at 4-30 A. M., and reached Kalu Khan's Fort at about 6 when I halted the troops and went forward to reconnoitre.

8. In order fully to understand what follows, a brief description of the country is necessary. Besud is a very small district lying in the angle between the Kabul and Kunar rivers. It is bounded on the north by a rang of hills separating it from the plain called the Dusht-i-Gamberi and from the rich valley of the Kunar. There are three main *tangis*, or passes, through these hills; the Maruf on the west, the Tokchi on the east along the right bank of the Kunar river, and the Paikob, about two miles west on the Tokchi, and separated from it by a high hill running north and south, and about four miles in length. The Tokchi Tangi is passable by infantry in single file, and cavalry can lead through it, though with some risk, as the path at one place is along a wooden aqueduct, four feet wide, overhanging the Kunar river. The Paikob Tangi presents no difficulties. The only portions of Besud that troops can act in are strips on the banks of the two rivers and the slopes at the foot of the

range of hills. The whole of the centre of the district is at this season under rice cultivation, and is an expanse of standing water and marsh, intersected by numerous deep watercourses, with ditches branching from them in all directions. To reach the foot of the hills the troops had to follow the left bank of the Kabul river for upwards of a mile, and then strike in single file along a winding path through swamp but bridged-over watercourses which eventually brought them out on the slopes towards the north-west corner of Besud, whilst the enemy were known to be towards the north-east corner. Hence it followed that our force was compelled to act upon a line perpendicular to its base (Dabela Kila and the bridge head), and to leave this uncovered. The enemy's left was as near our base as was our own right,—the marsh lying between the flanks of both forces and the bridge-head. It must, however, be borne in mind that, though this swamp was an obstacle that our troops could not pass, its difficulties were not insurmountable by an irregular enemy knowing every path and bye way in the country, and unencumbered with animals. It appeared to me quite probable that the enemy might detach a portion of their force to seize the bridge-head and attack Dabela Kila, so, having no troops to spare from my column, I sent back word to the officer commanding at Jellalabad to place the two guns of C.-3rd, Royal Artillery, at once in position on the right bank of the Kabul to cover the bridge-head, and to hold the latter in strength with troops from his garrison. As will be seen presently, the enemy were bent upon carrying out the very movement I was anticipating.

9. At about a mile to the east of Kalu Khan's Fort, a small and isolated hill rises out of the plain to a height of about fifty feet. Ascending this with a small escort, I saw the enemy in position about fifteen hundred yards distant. They were in line facing west, numbered 2,000 men with eighteen standards, and occupied some ruined forts and walled enclosures in the plain. Their right was in an old fort distant about 500 yards from the base of the hills. In

front of this was a dry ditch held by them in some force. Their left was in Bulandgarh, a village on the edge of the marsh, and along their line were banks, dry ditches, mounds and broken ground, affording excellent cover.

10. Having satisfied myself as to their position, I directed Colonel F. Dawson, 1st Madras Native Infantry, the next senior officer to myself, to bring up the troops and to place them in close formation behind and under cover of the hill, for the enemy were beginning to move in considerable numbers to their left, and I was anxious not to check a manœuvre which drew them from the hills. I learn from the Political Officer that as a matter of fact, they were absolutely ignorant that we had sufficient troops in Besud to take the offensive, and that they were even then on their way to the bridge-head and Dabela Kila, which latter they believed to be held by eighty men. This accounts for their leaving the very strong position on the *tangi* from which, later on, they were cut off by our cavalry. The Khan of Jellalabad and some of his retainers were with me on the hill ; also three or four officers and some sowars. We were seen by the enemy and mistaken for a reconnoitring party. As soon as they had taken ground some distance to their left, and had halted on descrying our troops, concealment was no longer possible, and I directed Colonel Dawson to form line of attack. This he did by extending a company each from the 5th Fusiliers on the left, the 1st Madras Native Infantry in the centre, and the 12th Foot on the right. The second companies of these corps were in support, and the third of the British troops, with the company of the 4th Madras Native Infantry, in reserve. The reserve company of the 5th Fusiliers was in *echellon* on the left, the cavalry line to the left rear of that again, to cover any attack through the Paikob Tangi on our flank, and to cut the enemy off from the hills should the opportunity present itself. The guns were kept till wanted behind the centre reserve. In this formation our force advanced until we were within 900 yards of the enemy's centre, and 600 to 700 yards from the fort on which their right

rested. Here the guns were brought into action, and infantry fire was directed upon the masses near the fort. The infantry had been cautioned immediately before coming into action to aim carefully. Their fire was remarkably steady and telling, and the bulk of the enemy's right being unable to face it, sped towards the hills.

11. News of this being brought to me, I ordered the cavalry to charge, and the Central India Horse at once swept along between the hills and the fort led by Lieutenant-Colonel Martin, and killed here, and in other parts of the field, twenty-five of the enemy. Some of the defenders of the fort, seeing their retreat cut off, stood their ground. There were twenty-two in all; of these, four were killed either just outside the fort or in the main enclosure, and eighteen retired into a loop holed tower at the south east corner. It was quite impossible to storm the tower as it then was, so the mountain guns were brought into the fort and opened at 30 yards range with double shell, cutting down the wall of the tower below the original entrance to within about four feet of the ground level.

12. The torment of these shells exploding in a tower only ten feet in diameter, goaded three of its inmates to charge out knife in hand. But in a small court-yard at the foot of the tower they were met by Color-Sergeant Woods, Private Openshaw, Lieutenant (Local Captain) H. Kilgour, and Lieutenant-Colonel T. Rowland, all of the 5th Fusiliers, and by Private Longworth, 12th Foot, when a desperate hand-to-hand fight ensued, in which the three Afghans were killed. Lieutenant-Colonel Rowland twice slightly, and Privates Openshaw and Longworth severely, wounded,— the first named Private receiving three deep knife-cuts. Whilst this was passing, a fire was being maintained from the tower, but no one knew how many of the enemy it held. As soon as the conflict in the court-yard had ended, Color-Sergeant Woods with dashing gallantry rushed up the *debris* and disappeared into the tower, closely followed by Captain Kilgour, and there these two found and slew five desperate

men at bay. A finer display of courage cannot well be imagined; and I do not hesitate to say that it deserves the highest reward that valour can obtain.

Fifteen of the enemy's dead were counted inside the tower, and it is probable more were hidden in the *debris,* which was so deep that two *jezails* were buried upright in it to within four inches of their muzzles.

13. Whilst this was going on, the few sabres of the Central India Horse that were present, a weak troop in all, had swept along the back of the fort down the enemy's line; but many of the latter had already been given refuge in the village of Besud by the very people we were protecting against them. Some were pursued by the cavalry to the banks of the Kunar river, and there slain or forced into its waters. Some, probably the majority, escaped by the Tokchi Tangi, or over the hills; and a few held the village of Beninga at the mouth of the *Tangi* and fired at our cavalry, but a beautifully pitched shell killed five, and the rest dispersed. In this dashing charge many deeds of valour were done by both officers and men. I can only regret that the swift-footedness of the enemy deprived these splendid horsemen of a fairer field for their powers.

14. It was now 10 o'clock, and the sun was exceedingly hot, so I took the troops back to Dabela Kila. Our casualties were few. One officer was slightly wounded, three privates severely amongst the British troops, a Native officer and two sowars in the cavalry. A nominal roll is appended. The Central India Horse had one horse killed, and five badly cut with knives. Fifty-three bodies of the enemy were counted by our officers in different parts of the field; whilst several more were seen to fall to the infantry fire at the beginning of the action, and to be carried way. I learn that their loss in killed alone is not less than seventy, and that many were wounded. When going through the Paikob Tangi, two days later, many traces of wounded were seen. Our expenditure of ammunition was small, only 19 shell and 1,572 rounds of shall-arm having been fired. Exclusive of

the Staff, there were actually engaged 24 British and 10 Native officers, and 674 fighting men of all arms.

15. The Political Officer having requested me to proceed to the fort of Abdul Khel to punish Sirdar Nizamudin Khan of that place for his open hostility to us on the 19th instant, I ordered the two guns of C-3rd, Royal Artillery, into Besud, and sent for a detachment of Madras Sappers and Miners from Rozabad. These latter arrived at Dabela Kila at midnight on the 19th, but there was neither Bickford's fuze nor blasting powder to be procured locally, so I was compelled to postpone further operations for a day. On the 20th some fuzes arrived by special messenger from Ali Boghan. Powder was procured by directing the Commissary of Ordnance to break up 300 nine-pr. service cartridges. I also reinforced the column with another troop of the Central India Horse.

These would have been useful in the plain beyond Besud, had the fort of Abdul Khel been held.

16. On the morning of the 21st the troops marched to Abdul Khel, a very strong fort, with six towers, at the northern entrance to the Tokchi Tangi. It had been held on the day of the action by about 300 men, but was now deserted. The distance to Abdul Khel from Dabela Kila by the Paikob Tangi—the route taken—is about nine miles. A party of the 5th Fusiliers was left to hold the heights between, and commanding the two passes, and one of cavalry to watch the undulating hills to the west of the Paikob. From these heights communication with Jellalabad could easily have been established had instruments been available. Here I desire to record that the want of signalling apparatus has been most severely felt. Although Dabela Kila is only a mile from Fort Sale, Jellalabad, there was no night communication between them for want of seviceable lamps.

17. At 8 A. M. the sappers began working at the towers. During the day about 1,000 ℔s. of gunpowder were found in one of the towers of the fort, so that only some 200 ℔s. of our own were used. At 2 P.M. I caused the whole of the season's crops of wheat and barley to be fired. These had

been cut and gathered ready for threshing but were still in
ear. At 3 the interior of the fort, which was handsomely
fitted up for such a place, was fired, and half an hour later
the six mines (which had been laid from outside) were
sprung. The destruction was complete. Sending the troops
back to Dabela Kila by the Paikob Tangi, I took a small
escort and returned myself by the Tokchi, passing the fort
of that name in flames. It and the cut crops around had
been fired earlier in the day by a small party of cavalry with
the Political Officer. The troops reached Dabela Kila
somewhat exhausted, for the march had been long and tir-
ing, and the heat very great. Here I would bring to notice
the excellent service done on this day by the twenty men of the
Madras Sappers and Miners under Lieutenant T. Digby, R.E.
This small party worked for seven hours hard and in-
cessantly, for the foundations of the towers were of stone
laid in mud, and were extremely difficult to undermine.
Such constant and severe work in excessive heat, and in
addition to a march of eighteen miles, shows an amount of
pluck and endurance which merits special mention. Lieutenant R. H. Brown, R.E., Assistant Field Engineer, Jellalabad, helped to supervise the work, and rendered valuable
assistance. During the operations of the 21st there was no
opposition. A few shots were, however, fired at our videttes
from a village on the left bank of the Kunar.

18. On the 22nd, at the request of the Political Officer,
I directed Lieutenant-Colonel Rowland, 5th Fusiliers, to
surprise Kila Banaras Khan, a fort in Besud belonging to
Mahomed Farukh, to fire it, and to bring in the owners prisoners. These directions were ably carried out by Lieutenant-Colonel Rowland, whose report accompanies these papers.
No opposition was offered. Mahomed Farukh had distributed powder and bullets amongst his people, and had collected
them ready to attack us in rear on the 19th instant in case
of reverse. Letters addressed to Mahomed Jan and other
leaders, were found in this fort.

19. On the 22nd the recrossing of the Kabul river began. During our sojourn in Besud, the water had been daily rising, and on the morning of this day it was found that two small foot bridges, thrown across shallow water between sandbanks, had been swept away. By that evening, however, the division of C-3rd, Royal Artillery, and the detachment of the 12th Foot had recrossed. The guns were at once placed in position to cover the passage, and so remained till it had been completed.

20. Dawn on the 23rd showed the Kabul a torrent. During the night the river had cut in behind the abutment of the bridge over its southern branch, and it became evident that a few inches more rise would carry away the whole structure. This actually happened a few hours after, and the portion of the force still in Besud had now to cross the whole breadth of the Kabul river in full flood—some 400 yards—and with a current estimated at not less than seven miles an hour. Twenty elephants and seven small rafts of skins were the means at hand. It became quite impossible to tow the rafts against the stream, and a question arose how much longer elephants could breast it. Indeed, I saw one of these animals forced back stern first by the current, unable even to hold his own against its force. In places where the elephants had to ford, the water was more than six feet deep. The rafts had to be taken out of the water at each trip and carried, some on men's heads, some on elephants, to the starting point half a mile up stream. Under these difficult conditions, the division of the mountain battery with all its mules, three troops of cavalry with all their horses and some of their ponies, the Detachment of Sappers and Miners, and some Madras Infantry, effected the passage. The guns were brought over on elephants. The saddlery, baggage, and some of the men came on rafts on elephants. The whole of the mules and horses, and all the baggage animals swam the 400 yards of river, in very many cases with their owners or drivers riding them or swimming alongsied. Some of the men of the

Central India Horse crossed as often as ten times this day to swim horses and ponies over; many crossed six and seven times. The men worked splendidly. Picked swimmers with ropes and unrolled turbans were placed down stream and did excellent service in rescuing exhausted men and animals.

But it was not to be expected that so dangerous a passage could be made without loss. A driver and a sowar's horse were, I regret to say, drowned.

21. On the 24th the remainder of the troop recrossed, 65 men of the 5th Fusiliers on the twenty elephants, being the last of all to leave Besud. I had sent some infantry to aid the guns in covering the retirement, but not a shot was fired.

22. It now only remains for me to make a few concluding observations.

I have to thank Colonel F. Dawson, 1st Madras Native Infantry, for the prompt and skilful manner in which he carried out my wishes as regards the disposition of the troops before and during the action of the 19th instant, as also for his aid and counsel throughout the expedition.

The handling of the cavalry left nothing to be desired. It reflects the highest credit for gallantry and skill upon Lieutenent-Colonel C. Martin, who commanded. It enabled us to inflict severe punishment upon the enemy.

My best acknowledgments are due to Major M. Protheroe, Political Officer, Jellalabad, not only for the accurate and reliable information he has always given me of the strength and movements of the enemy, but for his valuable aid in procuring rafts and boatmen, and for his cordial co-operation at all times.

To Major H. P. Pearson, my Brigade Major, I am specially indebted. It was on his observation and report of events in another part of the field that I ordered the cavalry charge which contributed so greatly to the success of the day. Major Pearson gave me the greatest assistance during the operations and proved himself then, as on all occasions, a most efficient Staff officer.

Major H. M. Buller, Central India Horse, pushed a reconnaissance on the 16th instant beyond Shigi in the Kunar Valley, and brought me informatin about the passes which proved most valuable.

The conduct of the troops during the operations in Besud merits my warmest thanks. Whatever they had to do they did well. Officers and soldiers, British and Native, Bengal and Madras, troops, all alike did admirably that which fell to them to do. Without tents they had to seek shelter where they might from the fierce heat of the May sun. The cheerfulness with which all ranks endured hardships and exposure, and the energy with which they laboured from dawn to dark during the passage of the Kabul, were equalled only by their steadiness in the field, and splendid courage where opportunity offered.

I enclose a sketch of the scene of action on the 19th instant, done on the ground by Captain J. E. Porteous, 4th Madras Native Infantry.

Nominal Roll of Casualties in action at Beninga (Besud) on the 19th of May 1880.

Major and Brevet Lieutenant Colonel Thomas Rowland, 5th Fusiliers, slight knife cut and bayonet wound in right hand; 1028 Private Frederick Snowling, 5th Fusiliers, severe deep gunshot wound, left thigh; 55 Private James Openshaw, 5th Fusiliers, three severe knife cuts, right forearm; 32nd Brigade 04 Private Jonathan Longwort, 12th Regiment, very severe deep knife cut, back of left shoulder, deep muscles severed; Jamadar Faim Khan, 1st Regiment C. I. H, left elbow joint cut through with knife, very severe; 993 Sowar Nand Singh, 1st Regiment C. I. H., severe, right calf of leg cut through with knife, very deep; 1090 Sowar Kadi Khan, 1st Regiment C. I. H., severe bullet wound over region of liver.

Brigadier General Doran and the Officers and men under his command, were thanked by the Governor General of India in Council, Sir Frederick Haines, Commander-in-Chief, General Sir Donald Stewart, and Major-General Bright, Commanding Khyber line force, for the judicious and successful manner in which they carried out the operations. During the absence of the Regiment across the river, the men of the 5th quartered in the fort, had a large amount of hard duty to perform, for in addition to their ordinary duties in the fort (which were very heavy) they had to find a large guard daily for the protection of the Regimental camp outside, and many of them were on duty several nights in succession. Before I go any further with this narrative I will bring forward—

The Fusiliers' Alphabet.

A is the Army in which we all serve,
  Second to none for endurance and nerve.
B is the batta most welcome to all,
  Whether their portion be great or be small.
C is our Colonel, a good man and true,
  Who treats all his men as a colonel should do.
D is the dangers, we each one have run,
  Since the year seventy-eight, when the war first begun.
E is our ememies—treacherous foes,
  Who seem to like plunder much better than blows.
F is our regiment, the Fifth Fusiliers,
  The pride of Old England, o'er two hundred years.
G stands for glory, of which there's not much,
  Unless fighting fleas and mosquitoes is such.
H is the hardship we all have gone through,
  Since we came to this country, Afghans to subdue.
I stands for the ills, in campaigning rife.
  In idleness felt, but forgotten in strife.
J is Jellalabad, a spot most accurst,
  Where heat, flies, and sandstorms, are all of the worst.
K stands for the killed, a list long and sad,
  If deaths from all causes, together we add.
L stand for the *lacs*, which the war it has cost,
  Also for the lives, which have through it been lost.
M is the medal, some day to be struck,
  And worn by all those, who to live have the luck.
N is the notion, we all entertain,
  That we could much better conduct the campaign.

O is the odour (not Rimmell nor Piesse),
   Of bullock, mule, camel—after decease.
P is the Post, which we anxiously wait,
   'Twill be welcome although 'tis a week or two late.
Q is the question, which o'ft does ascend,
   When is this blessed war going to end.
R is the rum, very seldom A 1,
   But still though diluted, 'tis better than none.
S stands for sickness, the worst of all woes,
   Which kills far more men than the knives of our foes.
T is our transport, at times very weak,
   Composed of mules, camels, and donkeys so meek.
U is our uniform simple-kirkie,
   Which at a mile distance, tis hard for to see.
V is the victories, that we have won,
   To gain which, each Soldier his duty well done.
W is the war, in which we're engaged,
   Which many folks think should have never been waged.
X the xpences, each man it has cost,
   To replace his clothing, worn out or got lost.
Y is the late Ameer Yacoob Khan,
   A man quite unfit to rule Afghanistan.
Z is the zeal, that the 5th always show,
   For the cause of their country, wherever they go.

On May 26th head-quarters and the three companies shifted their camp from near the fort to the Ameer's gardens, about two miles away, where, on arrival, they pitched, their tents and settled down. In these gardens are several well built and good sized buildings, which when first erected must have looked quite handsome. The main one is a fine circular shaped building, situated at the front of the gardens, from which a splendid view is obtained of the Kabul river, the surrounding country, and the snow clad mountains beyond. This building is the residence of the Ameer, who usualy spends the winter in Jellalabad, and so escapes the severer weather of Kabul. The gardens are protected on three sides by a high mud wall, and are also divided into several plots, by walls of the same material. These plots contain seneral fine lemon and lime orchards, and the roads and walks throughout the gardens are lined with handsome cyprus, fig, and other trees. There is also a fine large tank, about seven feet deep, in the centre of the garden, occupied by the Central Indian Horse, where all the troops, both British and Native, are allowed to bathe during the cool of the evening. Both the buildings and the gardens are going to ruin for want of looking after. If a few thousand rupees were spent in restoring them, they could be made into a right royal residence, of which even an English duke might be proud of. The weather in Jellalabad is now extremely hot, and those terrible hot winds and sandstorms visit us almost daily, sweeping across the land with intense force, like the simoon of the desert. The men stationed in the fort are troubled greatly by those awful plagues of flies, which seem to infest these parts ; and many of them no doubt often think of the words Josh Billings, who says, " its not the big, but the little things that trouble us, a man can dodge the elephant but he cant dodge a fly." An officer writing to the *Field* newspaper, describes Jellalabad as follows :—Jellalabad, where it was my fortune to be quartered for some time, is not exactly a paradise. Its hot winds and sand and dust storms are acknowledged to be unique, and its smells and flies are bad to beat. A westerly wind produces a combination of these plagues, which is about as much as the ordinary mind and body can stand ; and gives one an insight into the troubles of Pharaoh and his people. On June 1st, head-quarters and the 3 companies left the Ameers gardens and pitched their tents near the fort. At 3 a.m. next morning they marched (accompanied by a troop of the Central Indian Horse) in the direction of Ali Bogan. Passing this place they continued marching for about six miles further, when they halted on a piece of ground near the river, where they were shortly afterwards joined by a number of Her Majesty's 14th regiment and the 32nd Pioneers from Pesh Bolak. The object with which these troops were brought together, was to punish some tribes at the other side of the river, in the Kunar valley, for attacking and looting the convoys, and committing outrages on our people on the road between Elatchipore

and Jellalabad. On the following morning, June 3rd, the
force crossed the river on rafts ; and during the next 2 or 3
days were occupied blowing up the towers, and destroying
the villages of the offending tribes, who had fled on the
approach of our troops. During this time, the cavalry
scoured the valley in all directions, but could find no trace
of the delinquents. The work of destruction having been
completed, the troops recrossed the river on the afternoon
of the 6th. Next morning the force was broken up. The
troops from Pesh Bolak marching in the direction of that
place, and the 5th Fusiliers and the Central Indian Horse
marching to Ali Bogan, where they encamped for the day.
Next day the Fusiliers returned to Jellalabad, and again
pitched their tents and settled down in the Ameer's gardens.
Early on the morning after head-quarters and the three
companies left Jellalabad, June 3rd, on the expedition just
narrated, the Sudder Bazaar (which is about half a mile
from the fort, and which is occupied for the most part by
Hindoo and friendly Afghan shopkeepers) was attacked by
about 50 robbers, who belonged to the same tribe as stole
the cattle. The attack was made almost under the noses of
a Madrassee guard, consisting of 1 Sergeant, 1 Corporal,
and 12 Privates, who might, had they shown a bold front, have
driven off the thieves there and then. But the very man
who should have led them against the robbers, *i. e.* the
Sergeant, took to his heels and ran towards the fort, being
closely followed by one of the Privates. The Corporal who
should now have taken the Sergeant's place, stood still and
did nothing. A Private who had more presence of mind and
pluck in him than the Sergeant and Corporal put together,
now sprang forward, and calling on his comrades to follow
him, at once attacked the robbers, and managed after a
short time to kill 2 of them, wound 3 more, and put the
remainder to flight ; but not before they had killed 3 and
wounded 11 of the bazar people. The Private for this act
of gallantry was promoted to full Corporal. The Sergeant
and Private who ran away, were tried by Cout Martial, found

guilty, and sentenced ; the Sergeant to 50, and the Private to 25, lashes with the cat, and two years' imprisonment each ; at the expiration of which time they are both to be discharged from the army. For the next couple of weeks things went along very peaceably, the country round about Jellalabad being very quiet indeed. During this time our men were occupied with their usual duties of guards, pickets, &c. Those stationed in the Ameer's gardens, finding a large picket daily, for duty in the city, whose duty it was to prevent the camp followers (who were in the habit of going there to purchase provisions, vegetables, &c.) from being molested. This picket was anything but an agreeable duty, and very few men cared for it on account of the dreadful heat and the frightful stenches in the bazaars, which had to be patrolled by the sentrys throughout the day ; and as they are always crowded by a large and motley rabble of ruffianly Afghans, this was anything but an easy matter. Many of the Afghans who frequent the city are very fanatical, and it behoved the sentrys to keep their eyes about them, if only for their own sakes, as these gentlemen if they saw a favourable opportunity, would think very little of stabbing them in the back with their long and very sharp knives. The presence of this picket was not liked by the city people at all ; and it was nothing unusual as the sentrys were patrolling, for them to see the dark, cunning and treacherous looking faces of the shopkeepers scowling at them, and to hear their owners mutter in Pushto : Feringis, Kafirs, dogs, and many other epithets quite as complimentary. On several occasions, when I have been patrolling myself, the scowling faces of these Afghans, and their openly expressed hatred of us British (although they have a liking for our rupees), have put me in mind of a piece of poetry called the " Old Pindaree," which I think I cannot do better than bring before you. The verses are as follows :—

My father was an Afghan, and came from Candahar,
He rode with Nawab Ameer Khan, in the old Mahratta war.
From the Himalay to the Deccan, five hundred of one clan,
They asked no leave from king or chief, as they swept o'er Hin-
[dustan

My mother was a Braminee, but held to my father well,
  She was saved from the sack of Juleysur, when a thousand Hindoos
Her kindred died in the sally, so she followed where he went, [fell.
  And lived like a bold Pathanee, in the shade of a rider's tent.
Its many a year gone by now, but yet I often dream,
  Of a long dark march to the Jumna, and splashing across the stream.
The waning moon on the water, and the spears in the dim starlight,
  As I rode in front of my mother, and wondered at the sight.
But the British chased Ameer Khan, and the roving times must cease,
  My father got this village, and sowed his crops in peace.
But I was young and hot of blood—it was no life for me,
  So I took to the hills of Malwa, and became a Pindaree.
Praise to the name Almighty, there is no god but one,
  Mahomed is his prophet, and his will shall ever be done.
Ye shall take no use for money, nor your faith for lucre sell,
  Ye shall make no terms with the infidel, but smite his soul to hell.
Tell me ye men of Islam, who are living in slavish ease,
  Who wrangle before the Feringee for a poor man's last rupees.
Are ye better than were your fathers, who plundered with old Cheetoo?
  And squeezed the greedy traders. Don't traders now squeeze you?
Down there lives a mahajun—my father gave him a bill,
  I have paid the knave thrice over, and here I'm paying him still.
He shows me a long stamp paper, and must have my land—must he,
  If I were twenty years younger, he should get six feet by three.
And if I were forty years younger, and my life before me to choose,
  I wond'nt be lectured by Kafirs, or swindled by fat Hindoos.
But I'd go to some far off country, where Mossulmans still are men,
  Or take to the forest like Cheetoo, and die in a tiger's den.

Early on the morning of 23rd the camp of the 5th Fusiliers was aroused, and the men were ordered to pack their kits and strike the tents as soon as possible. This being done and a number of men having been told off to escort these things to the fort, the remainder of the regiment fell in and marched to the fort, where they were joined by a number of the Central Indian Horse. Brigadier General Doran having taken command, he ordered the force to march across the plain, in the direction of the Shinwarri country. The object with which the troops were going out, was to obtain the release of Kalu Khan, who had been made prisoner, together with all his escort, by the inhabitants of the villages of Daulatzie and Sangera, whilst out gathering revenue. The trops marched along until nearly midday, over a country which was a complete desert. The sun was extremely powerful, and as they could procure no water, they suffered dreadfully from heat and thirst. On their arriving within 3 or 4 miles of the villages they were met by Kalu Khan and his followers. It seems that as soon as the villagers who had made him a prisoner, got to know that a force was coming against them they released him and his people, and told them to go at the same time refusing to pay the taxes. Although the real object of the expedition had been achieved, Brigadier-General Doran said that but for the dreadful heat, and the exhausted nature of the men, he would go on and punish the villagers, and destroy their villages and crops. Water was now procured, and the troops were ordered to halt. Meanwhile the men who had been left behind in the Ameer's gardens to escort the tents and baggage to the fort, were, on their arrival there, ordered to wait for orders. About 7 A. M. these men were sent off in the same direction, as the troops under General Doran had taken before them. They were in charge of a number of mules laden with skins of water, and were ordered to join the above force as soon as they could. They had a terrible march across the plain and suffered dreadfully from the broiling heat of the sun : 2 men dying from heat apoplexy on the road. By the time they reached the column at 5 p. m., they were well nigh done up from exhaustion. Of the 2 men who died, one of them was a Private of the 5th, named Brand, and the other was a Native mule driver. Between 6 and 7 p. m. the troops were ordered to fall in, and directly afterwards commenced their march back towards Jellalabad, where they arrived thoroughly worn out, about 3 a. m. next morning. In the evening the poor fellow Brand was buried. On the 26th the 2 companies of the 5th, stationed in the fort, were relieved by 2 other companies from the Ameer's gardens. During the next 2 or 3 weeks things went along very quietly, the people round about giving little or no trouble, although many rumours were afloat of large gatherings in the Kunar Valley, at the other side of the Valley. Whether these rumours were true or not I cannot tell, but at any rate they never led to anything. On July 13th the city picket found daily by the 5th Fusiliers was discontinued, and the troops were ordered not to go into the city after that date, as the place was reeking with small pox and other diseases. On the 14th information was brought in that an Afghan chief, named Mogul Khan, had gathered a large number of tribesmen together at a place called Kila Mir Afzal in Girdab, which is a few miles from Elatchipore on the other side of the river, and was beginning to show his hatred of us by firing on our rafts as they passed down the river. It was decided to put a stop to Mr. Mogul Khan, by sending a force against him at once. The 5th Fusiliers were ordered to form part of this force, which was to leave Jellalabad on the 16th. The morning of the 16th came, and with it came the news that the expedition was cancelled. Why I cannot tell, but I heard that the guns from Elatchipore had given Mogul Khan a good peppering the day before. The cancelling of this expedition was not much regretted by our men, as the weather was so frightfully hot. On July 26th the two companies in the fort was relieved by two more from the gardens, and for the remainder of our stay in Jellalabad the tribesmen gave us no trouble. Although the surrounding country was pretty quiet, our men had still plenty of hard duty to perform in the shape of guards, pickets, &c. There is one thing I have forgotten to speak about so far, and that is the way that some of the Home papers go on about the way the British Soldier carries on in this country. According to some of them Tommy Atkins does nothing but torture the poor unoffending Afghans, and rob them of what they possess. In one instance I read where Tommy was charged with a far graver offence than either of the above. I think if some of these penny-a-liners, who write these things, would just take the trouble to come out here for a couple of weeks, and see for themselves how the British Soldiers really do carry on, they would have more praiseworthy things to say for them, and less pity for the poor, gentle, unoffending Afghans. An officer writing to one of the papers upon this subject, says :—From what I can make out from some of the Home papers the British Soldier in this country seems to be having rather a rosy time of it. His principal occupations appear to be the congenial ones of burning villages, looting the inhabitants, and committing other atrocites hitherto only attributed to the unspeakable Turks. One never knows when one is well off, and strange to say with all this he is not happy, and on reading the accounts of his doings is profane enough to say there is a mistake somewhere. His own ideas on the subject being connected more with dusty convoy work, endless marching, and counter marching in search of an enemy who so continually seems to vanish, that he has almost lost faith in his tangible existance. Probably if our kind friends, who find it so easy to write, would come and gain a little practical experience of the facts of the case they would be more lenient.

About July 20th it was rumoured that 3 or 4 days more would see peace proclaimed, and the war at an end. This rumour turned out to be true, for on the 22nd, at a Durbar held at Cabul by General Sir Donald Stewart, at which many influential Chiefs attended, Abdur Rahman, grandson of Dost Mohamed, was proclaimed Ameer. Mr. Lepel Griffin, the Chief Political Officer, in a speech, reminded that 3 months ago he stated that the armies of the British would withdraw as soon as the prospects of a settled administration were assured, and a chief acknowledged who should not only be friendly to the British, but have the cordial support of his own countrymen. Mr. Lepel Griffin continued : "since then Generals Stewart and Roberts and myself have endeavoured to carry into effect the wishes of the Government, and you are summoned to-day to hear that our efforts have been successful. The course of events having placed Abdur Rahman on the throne of Cabul, which fulfills the wishes and expectations of the Government, the Viceroy and the Government of the Queen Empress are pleased to announce that they publicly recognise Abdur Rahman, grandson of the illustrious Dost Mohamed, as Ameer of Cabul. It is to Government a source of satisfaction, that the tribes and chiefs have preferred a distinguished member of the Barakzai family, who is a renowned soldier, wise and experienced. His sentiments towards the British are most friendly, and as long as his rule shows that he is animated by these sentiments he cannot fail to receive the support of the British Government. He will best show his friendship to the British by treating as friends those subjects who have done us service. In accordance with the assurance already conveyed to you, the armies of The Queen Empress will shortly withdraw within those frontiers, decided by the Treaty of Gundamuck. We trust and firmly believe that your remembrance of the English will not be unkindly. We fought you in the field wherever you opposed us, but your religion has been in no way interfered with. Your honour and your women have been respected, and every one has been in secure possession of his property. Whatever has been necessary to support the army, has been liberally paid for. Since I came to Cabul I have been in daily intercourse with you, but I have never heard an Afghan make a complaint against the conduct of any soldier, English or Native, belonging to Her Majesty's Army. The British Government has always been well disposed towards Afghanistan. You all know how it supported and assisted the former rulers of the country. It has no other wish than your happiness and prosperity, and it is with this object alone that to-day it recognises Sirdar Abdur Rahman as Ameer of Cabul." Although the war was now at an end we did not expect to leave Afghanistan until September, as the weather was almost too hot for marching, but for some cause or other the Government ordered the troops to retire to India as soon as possible. Accordingly on the 10th of August we left the Ameer's gardens, and encamped near the fort. Early next morning having been joined by the two companies from the fort. We marched out of Jellalabad and commenced our journey towards India. On arriving at Ali Bogan we halted for the day. Next day we marched to Elatchipore, and next day (the 13th) to Chardeh, 14th to Basawal, 15th to Dhakka, 16th to Lundi Khana, 17th to Kata Koostea, and on the 18th to Shaghai heights, passing through Ali Musjid, which has been wonderfully improved. Barracks have been erected, new roads made, and Martello towers built on the tops of all the surrounding hills. Leaving Shaghai on the 19th we marched along for a few miles and passed out of the Khyber Pass and through Jumrood, and a couple of hours afterwards, had crossed the old frontier, left Afghanistan behind, and were encamped at Harri Singh. . During this march from Jellalabad, many dead transport animals were passed on the road, and as a consequence, our long suffering nasal organs, were often saluted by the sweet odour of that delicate perfume, called " Essence of Camel." The march was also a very hot one, but very few men fell out on the road, and although 60 or 80 were invalid from Jellalabad to India, we were said to be one of the healthiest regiments at the front, having had less sickness and lost fewer men from disease during the campaign than any other regiment on the Khyber line. The reason of this was no doubt owing to the majority of our men being old and seasoned Soldiers ; men who have braved the climate and dangers of India for many a long year. The number of men we have lost by death, from all causes, is thirteen. The names of these men are as follows :—

PRIVATES.	C. SHIELDS.	R. BRAND.
E. MILLER.	W. BURROWS.	R. LEGGETT.
J. HERRING.	W. DICKISON.	W. DUDLEY.
M. HYNES.	T. CAIN.	M. FOLEY.
J. BERKS.	J. ADCOCK.	

They should have died in their own loved land,
  With friends and kinsmen near them.
Not withered thus on a foreign strand,
  With no thought, save heaven to cheer them.
What recks it now is their sleepless sound,
  In the port where the wild waves swept them.
Than if Home's green turf, their graves had bound,
  Or the hearts they loved had wept them.

Then why repine, can they feel the rays
  That pestilent sun sheds o'er them.
Or share the grief, that must cloud the days,
  Of the friends who now deplore them.
No ! their barque's at anchor ; its sails are furled.
  It hath 'scaped the storm's deep chiding.
And safe from the buffeting waves of the world,
  In a haven of peace is riding.

Leaving Hurri Singh next morning (the 20th), we marched to Peshawar, where we halted a day to rest the baggage animals.   On the 22nd we left Peshawar, and marched day after day until we arrived at Klyrabad, which is on the side of the river Indus.   It was thought we should have to stay here for several days, as the bridge of boats had been washed away ; but a number of flats having been got together, we crossed over on these next morning and continued our march to Lawrencepore, where we arrived on the 28th.   Here we were ordered to halt until further orders. Two days afterwards (August 30th), we were joined by the companies from Gundamuck, who had had during their stay there a deal of hard duty to perform ; and many of the men had suffered much from fever and dysentry.   A few days after our arrival in Lawrencepore, it came out in orders that the 5th Fusiliers would proceed to England during the ensuing trooping season, which was good news for the majority of the men who have been many years in the country.   The regiment has been on the verge of going home for several years, but as has been seen it has not

done so. But that it will go home very shortly there
is not the slightest doubt, as it is, with one exception, the
oldest European regiment in India ; and when this comes
to pass each Fusilier can exclaim : At last! at last! oh at
last! I will now bring this account of "What the Fusiliers
Did " during the Afghan campaigns of 1878-79 and 1879-80
to a close, hoping that what I have written may not have been
uninteresting to those who have read it. It is now September 22nd, and we are still in Lawrencepore; but each one of
us expects—

Within a few short days from now, from here to march away
  To Jhelum, where we'll take the train and journey to Bombay,
And then aboard a gallant barque we very soon will be,
  And quickly will commence our voyage across the briny sea.

And as the ship leaves port, and sails from India's burning clime,
  The band will then strike up, and play a farewell Auld lang Syne,
And then for several weeks across the ocean's raging foam,
  We'll sail along until we reach Old England, Home, Sweet Home.

And when at Portsmouth town we land, we'll give three hearty cheers,
  And many friends will come to greet the war-stained Fusiliers.
Then each man will a furlough get, and journey home lighthearted,
  And then will meet dear ones from whom for years he has been
                                                      [parted.
Should the honour of our nation, at any future day
  Be threatened by some foreign power, at home or far away,
Let England then call on the 5th : the call will not be vain, [main.
  For 'gainst her foes, where'er they be, we'll fight with might and

We'll always strike, for God and right, and make our foemen reel,
  And to our country's cause remain for ever true as steel.
We'll never give up mortal foes give up our arms and yield,
  But fight until the last, and die like heroes on the field.

For are we not Brittania's sons, our country's boast and pride,
  The men who have for nigh two years the Afghan host defied.
The men who always have stood firm amid the battle's fray,
  The men who have their foemen beat on many a well fought day
                                                      [plain,
The men who many a storm have braved, on mountain and on
  The men who always have been staunch, and always will remain,
Then let Old England rest assured, in wars of future years,
  She always may depend upon the Gallant Fusiliers.

                    THE END.